THE
PUBLIC RELATIONS
WRITER'S HANDBOOK

THE
PUBLIC RELATIONS
WRITER'S HANDBOOK

Merry Aronson • *Don Spetner*

LEXINGTON BOOKS
An Imprint of Macmillan, Inc.
NEW YORK
Maxwell Macmillan Canada
TORONTO
Maxwell Macmillan International
NEW YORK   OXFORD   SINGAPORE   SYDNEY

Library of Congress Cataloging-in-Publication Data

Aronson, Merry.
   The public relations writer's handbook / Aronson & Spetner.
   p. cm.
   ISBN 0-02-901052-7
   1. Public Relations.   2. Public relations—Authorship.
3. Publicity.   I. Spetner.   II. Title.
HV6626.2.B27 1993
659.2—dc20   93-18619
                                                            CIP

Lexington Books
An Imprint of Macmillan, Inc.
866 Third Avenue, New York, N.Y. 10022

Maxwell Macmillan Canada, Inc.
1200 Eglinton Avenue East
Suite 200
Don Mills, Ontario M3C 3N1

Macmillan, Inc. is part of the Maxwell Communication
Group of Companies.

Printed in the United States of America

printing number

1 2 3 4 5 6 7 8 9 10

This book is dedicated to my mother and father, Jeanne and Zola Aronson, who gave me, among many other gifts, a profound love and respect for the English language; and to David M. Rubin and Richard Petrow, who asked me to teach and thought I had something to say. God bless 'em.
—M.A.

To Laurie, Jamie, and Michael, for being there every day for me; and to Buddy and Lil, for teaching me the value of hard work, honesty, and focus.
—D.S.

Contents

Introduction

Today more than ever, the role of public relations is evident in everything, from informing the public about political candidates to educating teenagers on safe sex to encouraging economic development in deprived areas at home and abroad. Public relations professionals hope to shape opinions and, more importantly, influence actions ranging from consumer spending to new legislation. And good writing is always at the core of effective public relations.

A successful professional must have the skill to communicate ideas, information, and emotions. Clear, concise, accurate, and credible, a professional must be able to write in many styles, tones, and voices, for many different audiences. The public relations writer often functions as a ghostwriter for others, such as a company's chief executive officer and other members of senior management. Trade publications may run well-written news releases under their own reporters' bylines, making few, if any, changes.

Working on a tight deadline as a provider of background information, facts, details, and access to interviews or credible news sources, the public relations professional serves as an invaluable link in the chain between the client or company and media coverage.

Meeting these demands requires a respect for truth and accuracy and adherence to a rigorous ethical code. While always acting as an advocate for the client or company and always having a specific point of view, the true professional does not exaggerate, equivocate, or misrepresent the facts. Ultimately, the success of one's ongoing relationships with members of the media is built on consistent credibility and reliability.

To help public relations writers achieve their professional goals, this book offers a simple, step-by-step approach to creating a wide range of documents, from basic news releases, pitch letters, biographies, and media alerts to more complex and sophisticated speeches, media campaign proposals, crisis responses, and in-house publications. Examples from successful public relations campaigns and hypothetical cases illustrate the fundamentals, as well as some possible flourishes.

For working professionals who do not have a newswriting background or those who have discovered a gap in their writing repertoire, this book is a resource to be opened at whatever chapter might apply to the writing assignment at hand.

For students aspiring to enter the field, this is a how-to book, best followed in sequence. For those with no news or public relations background—volunteers with charitable organizations or public affairs and information officers in government agencies—the technical discussions here are plain enough to be easily understood and followed.

We do not claim to have all the solutions to the demands of public relations writing. Drawing on our combined thirty years of experience at world-famous companies and public relations agencies, our work with students, and our conversations with fellow writers, however, we are offering you our secrets to cracking the public relations writing barriers and getting your message heard by as wide a public as possible. We were motivated to develop this book because we could find no others on the market that approached the same topics as simply and practically as we have here.

Our experience as working professionals and as leaders of seminars on public relations writing has convinced us of one fact: We can all use a manual that reminds us of the essential steps and offers models for completing complex assignments.

For their help in bringing this manual to fruition, we would particularly like to acknowledge the responsiveness of our editor, Beth Anderson, and the invaluable help and support of Carol Ames, Barbara Aronson, Emily Aronson, Ted R. Aronson, Theo, Natalie, and Sam Aronson, Howard Bloom, Margaret Brennan, Gene Busnar, Tom Colbert, Hugh Connor, Frank Cowan, John E. Cox, Jr., Cheryl Daly, Les Davis, Donald C. Farber, Carl Folta, Laurie Friedman, David Glazer, William Golightly, Rolf Gompertz, Laurie Goodman, Jodi Heimler, Josephine Hemsing, Jeff Herman, Rob Jacobsen, Marc Kirkeby, Dalina Soto-Loeser, Nansea McDermott, Bob Meyer, Tom Mignanelli, Bernie Mogelever, NBC's Department of Media Relations and Corporate Communications, New York University's Department of Journalism and Mass Communications, Sam Nishikawa, The Nissan Corporate Communications Department, Norio Ohsawa, Geof Prysirr, Rick T. Reed, Maxim Rohowsky, Peter Rohowsky, Barry Schwartz, Howard Shenson, Karen Sherry, Ken Shimba, Deborah Sole, Paul Spindler, UCLA's Extension Program, David Weinstein, Norman Weissman, Frank White, Burt Wolf, Tak Yamada, and Irwin Zwilling. Our immeasurable gratitude also goes to the many dozens of reporters, editors, producers, and public relations executives who generously shared their time and knowledge with us.

Be advised that this book will not tell you everything you will ever need to know about public relations. It is narrowly focused on writing. We disagree with those who feel that writing is strictly an inborn talent that cannot be taught. Good writing is born of many factors, such as clear thinking, avid reading and—most elusive of all—original, imaginative ideas. It also draws on many basic skills that can be practiced and honed. The writing process can be simplified and demystified, so that skills can be improved and talent developed. While no book alone can impart all of these qualities to its readers, this book will provide each reader and writer with a strong foundation for successful public relations writing.

1

The News Release

Making Your Story Newsworthy

Many published news and feature stories originate from news releases, the most common form of public relations writing. Also called press releases, news releases announce a client's news or publicize its products or services.

Almost 60 percent of the editorial contents of the *New York Times* and *Washington Post* are generated by public relations efforts, according to a classic study that analyzed the editorial contents of those newspapers.[1] Today, news releases, press conferences, official proceedings, and other nonspontaneous events continue to make major contributions to news coverage in these two large, well-respected newspapers. In smaller newspapers, the percentage of nonspontaneous material is even higher.

Journalists are inundated by dozens of news releases every day. If your release is to be read and considered for coverage, it must offer a newsworthy story, stated clearly and simply, long on information and short on adjectives. A news release typically announces a staff change; introduces a new product, service, or idea; reports new findings from a survey; alerts the media to an upcoming event; or simply presents new information. Sometimes a release is the basis of an entire story. At other times, an idea in it suggests a related story or affects a story an editor or reporter already has in progress.

To write a good news release, first you must understand what it is about your subject that is important. Then you must know how to summarize that information at the beginning of the release, quickly

[1]Leon V. Sigal, *Reporters and Officials, The Organization and Politics of Newsmaking* (Lexington, Mass.: D.C. Heath and Company, 1973), 121.

back up the lead statement with facts, and save the less important details for last. This is known as the inverted-pyramid style of newswriting. The most comprehensive information is put in the lead, so that the reader gets the point of the story even if he or she reads only the first sentence or paragraph.

A press release must be a complete story, because some publications will run a release verbatim. This is usually more true of trade publications. Publications for larger audiences generally have larger staffs and allow their reporters more time for further reporting and rewriting.

Trade vs. Consumer Press

Print journalism comprises two categories, trade and consumer. A trade publication is one that is intended for a specific profession or industry. For example, *Entree* is a trade publication for the food business; *Firehouse* is a trade magazine for fire fighters; *Variety* is a trade newspaper for the entertainment industry; and *Women's Wear Daily* is a trade publication for the fashion field.

Consumer press is designed for the general reader. Like *Women's Wear Daily*, *Vogue* magazine is devoted primarily to fashion, but it is a consumer magazine. Its market is readers with a general interest in fashion, not fashion professionals. *Newsweek, Time,* and *People* are also consumer publications. Local newspapers such as the *St. Louis Post-Dispatch,* the *Chicago Tribune,* the *Knoxville Journal,* and the *Fort Worth Star Telegram* are all consumer publications.

Broadcast programs usually fall into the consumer category, although cable television has introduced the concept of "narrowcasting," or targeting audiences with specific interests. But most TV and radio news programs are for consumer viewers and listeners—people of varied ages and backgrounds, with different hobbies and jobs.

Regardless of the client you represent and the industry you work in, you yourself are also a consumer, a representative of the lay audience. When judging a story for its value to the trade and consumer press, use *yourself* as a yardstick to measure consumer interest in the story: Do *you* care about it, as a nonindustry member? Does it affect *your* life—or that of your neighbors and friends—outside of your business? Does the information stand out from the ordinary to *you?*

When you can answer yes to these questions, you may have a release for the consumer press.

A news release to consumer media should be easily understood by the general reader.

The style of a trade release, on the other hand, can use technical terms that are in common use in a particular profession or trade, terms that might not be understood by a general audience.

In public relations, you must constantly analyze your own stories and decide if they are appropriate for the trade press, the consumer press, or both. Rarely, if ever, will you have a story only for the consumer press, but you may often have releases that will interest only the trades.

Before You Write

Ask yourself the following questions *before* you prepare a release:

- Is this story *truly* newsworthy, and will it interest the intended audience? Much has been written on the subject of what is news and what should be covered. Some say news is anything people didn't know about yesterday or anything that affects their lives. The late newspaper columnist Walter Winchell used to say that news is anything that protrudes from the ordinary. While the debate about judging news value is sure to continue as long as news is reported, you can begin to measure the news value of your story by asking if it offers any significant information that was not available before and whether anybody will care.
- Does this story answer all the questions it is likely to raise?
- Will this story, if covered, advance my client's objectives?
- Are all the facts and figures in the story 100 percent accurate? Has every name, date, and piece of information been double-checked with a reliable source?

When the answer is yes to every question on the list above, you are ready to write the first draft of a press release. When the answer is no, it is probably not appropriate for you to issue a release. There may be times when you will advise your client against putting out a release until the story warrants one. Every time you send a "non-story" to a journalist, you weaken your credibility as a public relations representative, and you also waste your client's time and money.

Research

As with all effective public relations writing, the first step in preparing a news release is to research the story. Learn as much as you can about the subject of the release. For example, if you're writing about a product, study its development and use the product yourself. If you're writing about a television program, watch it and learn about its background and production. If you're writing about a survey or a book, read it carefully, and perhaps talk to the surveyor or author. If you're announcing an event, familiarize yourself with all available details—even those you will not include in the release. Some of this research is done by talking to the people involved, informally interviewing them to gather background information, gain insight, and focus perspective.

As a public relations writer, you are likely to be privy to all or most of the information and background on the subject you are representing, but some of that information may not be for immediate or even eventual disclosure. If you are ever uncertain, make sure to ask what information is for release and what is not.

Your research for writing a news release should also include checking the files to see how similar releases were handled, and where and how they were covered by the media. Also review any existing material that could illuminate your topic.

Content

Outline the release before you write it to ensure a clear and logical flow of information. Try to limit the release to one or two pages. Also, make sure to define technical terms used and to attribute announcements to officials. If the story lends itself to humorous interpretation, let the reporter have fun with it. You should present the story in a straightforward manner.

News releases can be divided into two categories: hard news and soft (or feature) stories. Thousands of subjects are covered in press releases, from free lunches offered at the local YMCA to multibillion-dollar corporate takeovers. Typical hard news releases cover such areas as personnel appointments; new products, companies, and services; events; and survey results. Feature story releases typically cover such areas as trends, human interest items, and ongoing projects.

Let's take a look at a common release and review how it is structured and written.

The Appointment Release

Companies hire, fire, and promote people all the time. News releases on personnel changes are thus frequently required, and they are structured this way:

1. State the appointee's name and title, and attribute the announcement to an official from the company. Also state the name of the person to whom the appointee will report and when the appointment becomes effective. (If this last fact is not included, it is implied that the appointment is effective immediately.)
2. State the scope of the appointee's responsibilities in relation to the company or client, and describe the nature of the business. Sometimes a quotation from the appointee's boss is used in this second paragraph; rarely, however, is the quotation used by the press—thereby making it optional and for the most part unnecessary.
3. State the appointee's professional and educational history and perhaps offer a few personal facts, such as his or her place of residence, place of origin, and, sometimes, marital status.
4. State the name of the person being replaced *(optional; it may be a touchy subject)*, or, if the position is new, say that the subject of the release "has been appointed to the newly created position of . . . "

Notice that an appointment release first focuses on the responsibilities of the appointee and the business the appointee works for; only after these have been established is the appointee's background brought in. Here's a hypothetical appointment release, written in paragraph form:

NICHOLAS ADDAMS APPOINTED VICE-PRESIDENT, PRODUCT DEVELOPMENT, ABC ELECTRIC

[CITY, month, date]—Dr. Nicholas H. Addams has been named Vice-President of Product Development for ABC Electric, effective July 6. The appointment was announced today by Jason Snoapes, Senior Vice-President, Product Development and Acquisitions, ABC Electric.

Addams succeeds Raymond Barnes, who earlier this month announced his intention to retire from the company.

Addams, who will be based in ABC Electric's headquarters in Passaic, New Jersey, will be responsible for approving and supervising the design and production of all products to be developed by ABC Electric for consumer and industrial use.

Snoapes said, "Having to replace someone with the experience and industry savvy of Ray Barnes would be an enormous challenge to any company, but we were extremely fortunate to have a natural successor within our own ranks. With his background in engineering and his firsthand experience working on some of the most innovative technological developments of the past decade, Nick Addams has already demonstrated an ability to keep ABC Electric's 'homegrown' products on top in the marketplace as we move ahead in the 1990s."

Previously, Addams had been the director of Consumer Products Development since June 1987. In that position, he coordinated the development of various electronic home conveniences—including breakthrough voice-activated home heating and lighting systems—as well as ABC Electric's popular home security systems, invisible fences, and audiovisual home entertainment centers.

From February 1982 until May 1987, Addams was special-projects director for ABC Electric's international division.

Addams came to ABC Electric from the New York industrial electronics company Omega Development, Inc., where he had been a design manager in the factory equipment division from January 1980 until January 1982. While serving in that role, he also became involved in the marketing end of the industry, by working as a technical planner, adviser, and lecturer at Omega's semiannual trade shows. From October 1978 until December 1980, he was the engineering manager in the robotics department, where he had started with the company as an engineer in February 1976.

A 1975 graduate of the Massachusetts Institute of Technology with a doctorate in mechanical engineering, Addams earlier received an M.S. degree in computer science (1971) and a B.S. degree in physics (1969) from Rensselaer Polytechnic Institute in his native Troy, New York.

Addams lives in Fort Lee, New Jersey, with his wife, Hillary.

CONTACT: John Doe, ABC Electric Publicity, (202) 555–1234.
ABC Electric, [month, date, year]

The Lead

The lead of a news release is all-important and should read like the lead of a news story. All the essential information summarizing the whole story should be contained in the first paragraph.

When Hill & Knowlton, the public relations agency representing Welch Foods, announced a new product line, the lead of the press release was written this way.

WELCH FOODS INTRODUCES NEW LINE
OF ALL-NATURAL FROZEN JUICES

[CITY, month, date]—Welch Foods has announced it will market a new selection of all-natural frozen juice concentrates that will be available to consumers in supermarkets this November. The new Welch's Orchard 100 percent Natural Frozen Concentrate products include three tangy flavors—Grape, Apple-Grape, and Harvest Juice Blend.

Welch's new line of fruit juices is a trade news story until it's available to consumers in the market, at which time food and nutrition editors in the consumer media might want to write about it too.

The expansion of product lines is also usually trade news, and here's a lead paragraph from a representative press release prepared by Bozell, Jacobs, Kenyon & Ekhardt, the public relations firm representing Ingersoll-Rand Company:

INGERSOLL-RAND EXPANDS AIR-HAMMER LINE

[CITY, month, date]—Ingersoll-Rand Company has expanded its air-hammer line for professional mechanics in automotive, fleet, body shop, and general purposes maintenance. Three new models have been added to the existing two-model line. All models have an alloy steel barrel and a heat-treated piston.

Both of these releases go on to elaborate on the attributes of the products and give the reasons for their development.

When Intersource Technologies and the American Electric Power Company unveiled their plans to reproduce a new type of light bulb, the lead paragraph of their news release was constructed this way:

NEW LIGHTING TECHNOLOGY UNVEILED
AT EDISON ELECTRIC INSTITUTE MEETING

[CITY, month, date]—A new lighting technology for residential and commercial use was unveiled here today in a joint announcement by Intersource Technologies and American Electric Power Company, Inc.

The electronic light bulb, known as the E-Lamp, is a long-burning bulb designed to combine the compactness and light intensity of incandescent bulbs with the energy efficiency of fluorescent lamps. "This is an entirely new generation of lighting technology that we plan to have available in early 1993," said Pierre G. Villere, president of Intersource, developer of the new technology. "We believe it can change the entire lighting industry."

Villere said the E-Lamp is "four times as efficient" as an incandescent bulb "with identical lighting output." He added that the bulb has no filament to burn out over its 20,000-hour life. "It just dims gradually as the phosphor coating of its globe ages," he said.

Here's an example of a feature story press release announcing a new television show hosted by the legendary Roy Rogers and Dale Evans. With more than ninety-one films to his credit, twenty-two books to hers, and a slew of other achievements, distinctions, and awards, there were any number of ways to introduce the famed couple. But the important news here to both the client (The Nashville Network) and the audience (trade and consumer press) was that

Roy and Dale were back on television after a long absence. And so the lead of the announcement release was written this way:

FOR IMMEDIATE RELEASE
ROY ROGERS AND DALE EVANS COHOST NEW SERIES
ON THE NASHVILLE NETWORK

"Happy Trails Theatre" Debuts January 4

NASHVILLE, November 20—After more than twenty years since their last full-season TV series, the King of the Cowboys and the Queen of the West are returning to television in a weekend series premiering on The Nashville Network (TNN) on Saturday, January 4, 1986.

Remaining faithful to the inverted pyramid, the release continues with each paragraph supplementing the story with less essential information. This form allows an editor to cut the release after any complete paragraph and retain the most important information of the story:

Titled "Happy Trails Theatre," the ninety-minute program is hosted by Roy Rogers and Dale Evans and features films from their treasure chest of classic Westerns. Each show, airing Saturdays at 5:00 P.M. (it can also be seen at 11:00 A.M. and 12:30 A.M., all times Eastern), opens and closes with Roy and Dale sharing personal anecdotes about how the featured film was made and the events happening in their private lives at the time.

"Happy Trails Theatre" presents films made between 1938 and 1948, and includes the first movie Roy and Dale ever made together, "Cowboy and the Señorita" (1944), and Roy's own personal favorite, "Under Western Stars," which launched his legendary singing-cowboy career in 1938.

Renowned actors Gabby Hayes, Smiley Burnette and Andy Devine figure in many of the films showcased, and Roy's beloved "acting partner," Trigger, appears in most of the movies as well. Nostalgia buffs will immediately recognize the new series' theme song, "Happy Trails," which was written by Dale.

"We feel delightfully nostalgic doing this program," says Roy. "We haven't seen some of these films in over forty years—and some of them we never did see."

Among the many tales Roy and Dale tell of their Hollywood days are stories of how Roy became King of the Cowboys (this honor was achieved when he ranked as the number-one Western movie star, a position he held for thirteen consecutive years from 1943 to 1955); why stuntmen are the unsung heroes of the industry (sometimes they suffered more than just clipped jaws and chipped teeth); and how the blizzard of '47 almost canceled their wedding in Oklahoma.

They also show photos never seen by the public before, and Roy wears some of his original custom-made Western wardrobe from his early movie roles. His authentic costumes were just one of the distinctions that made many of Roy's films period pieces, such as "Colorado" (1940), which was set in the American Civil War, and "Rough Riders Roundup" (1930), whose backdrop was the Spanish-American War. Roy made a total of ninety-one films in his career.

David Hall, the vice-president and general manager of TNN, remarked: "We are excited about bringing "Happy Trails Theatre" to The Nashville Network. Having recently celebrated their fiftieth year in show business, Roy Rogers and Dale Evans have few rivals in terms of versatility and longevity. Their films largely shaped the Western prototype, for years a favorite of moviegoers, and continued to attract large audiences on television."

In addition to films, Roy has been a major figure on radio, television, and records to several generations. He and Dale have recorded over 400 songs, and their newest album, "Many Happy Trails," was recorded in Nashville this year. Roy Rogers comic books and comic strips are still in worldwide syndication, and he and Dale have broken dozens of box-office records at rodeos and state fairs nationwide. Over 400 products were licensed by the Roy Rogers name and image, and Victorville, California, is the site of the Roy Rogers–Dale Evans Museum, the largest museum built and owned by any entertainer, which exhibits memorabilia from their personal and professional lives.

"Happy Trails Theatre" is produced by Ross K. Bagwell, Sr., and directed by Ross K. Bagwell, Jr., for Cinetel Productions in Knoxville, Tennessee. The associate producers are Packy Smith and Patrick Leigh-Bell.

The Nashville Network is the entertainment service with country-music emphasis. Just two years old, TNN is now seen in more than 24.1 million cable television households and is one of the fastest-growing network entertainment services. Programming for this eighteen-hours-a-day, advertiser-supported service is produced by The Nashville Network, a division of Opryland USA, Inc., of Nashville, Tennessee; marketing and distribution functions are handled by Group W Satellite Communications of Stamford, Connecticut.

[Date code]
For further information, contact [name, phone number].

Because The Nashville Network is a cable service available nationwide, this release is relevant to media across the country. But a good way to localize this story would be to inform each editor of what specific channel carries The Nashville Network in his or her area. Thus, the new lead, localized to the Milwaukee area, could be written this way:

FOR IMMEDIATE RELEASE
ROY ROGERS AND DALE EVANS COHOST NEW SERIES
ON THE NASHVILLE NETWORK
"Happy Trails Theatre" Debuts January 4

NASHVILLE, November 20—After more than twenty years since their last full-season TV series, the King of the Cowboys and the Queen of the West are returning to television in a weekend series premiering on the Nashville Network (TNN) on Saturday, January 4, 1986. The Nashville Network can be seen in Milwaukee on Channel 10.

The U.S. Fire Administration wrote a sample press release for distribution to firehouses nationwide. Each fire-fighting organization was to fill in the blanks to localize the release for its particular area, before sending it to the local media. Here is that release:

Fire Fighters: fill in blanks with local information.

(Organization letterhead)

For Immediate Release

Contact name:
Address:
Telephone:
Date:

(City), (state). (Name) announced today that *(your fire organization)* is launching a public education program— *Let's Retire Fire*—to educate older Americans about fire safety. This program is part of a national effort to reduce senior citizens' injuries and deaths by fire and is sponsored by the Federal Emergency Management Agency's U.S. Fire Administration.

Unfortunately, the United States has one of the highest fire death rates in the industrialized world. And our older Americans are at the highest risk of fire-related deaths—double that of the rest of the population. Every year more than 1,300 Americans sixty-five and over die in fires. These fire deaths and injuries are tragic but preventable.

Let's Retire Fire teaches senior citizens simple steps to combat fire hazards. To get these safety messages out, *(organization)* will run local print and radio public service announcements and will distribute home safety checklists to senior citizens in the area.

Observed *(name)*, *(title)*, "This is one of the best opportunities we have to make a real impact on the senior citizen fire problem in our area. Last year alone, we lost *(number)* people and/or *(dollar amount)* in property, needlessly. If we all become partners to combat this fire problem, we'd probably reduce senior citizen fires by more than half.

"I think that's a commitment worth making, and that's why we're cooperating wholeheartedly with the U.S. Fire Administration on this effort. We're going to do our best, with the community's help, to turn our senior citizen fire problem around."

Just as in feature news stories, press releases intended as soft news, or features, often make use of the delayed lead. That is, the specific subject of the story doesn't come into clear focus until a few paragraphs into the piece, after the lead sets the background and tone. Here's an example of a delayed lead in a release about a new robot called Maxx Steele. It begins by addressing trends in the toy and robot industries and gets to the exact subject in the fourth paragraph:

ALL IN THE (ROBOT) FAMILY

[CITY, month, date]—Last year it was Cabbage Patch dolls. This year, it appears that families all over America will be adopting robots.

Thanks to modern technology and the fertile imaginations of toy-industry designers and engineers, today's robots have more than sophisticated electronic circuitry: They have personality.

Yes, there are still many thousands of faceless robots toiling in factories (and even doing high-risk police work) throughout the world. But "friendly" robots are quite something else, and they are fast becoming integral members of our nation's households.

According to Fred D'Ignazio, author of many articles on robots and high technology, this comes as no surprise. "The public has long been ready for the friendly, personal robots," says D'Ignazio, "because they illustrate the natural marriage between technology and creativity and are the ideal playthings for the entire computer-age family." Indeed, D'Ignazio and his family have "adopted" a two-foot-tall robot of their very own—"Maxx Steele"— and Fred reports that his two children treat him "as more of a pet or a pal than an appliance."

The release goes on to describe the various functions the robot can perform and its recommended retail cost.

Here is another example of a feature release with a delayed lead:

STAR PROBLEMS? CALL "BUBBLES," THE BABY WRANGLER

Baby Boom Prop Master Jimmy Wagner and His Bag of Tricks

[CITY, month, date]—In the midst of a blistery cold Vermont winter, production on a multimillion-dollar film was stalled on the very first day. Cameras were set. The crew was ready. Everything waited on the star, who at that moment was sobbing uncontrollably. It was a job for Jimmy Wagner.

The film was the hugely successful feature *Baby Boom*. The star, actually stars, were three-year-old twins Kristina and Michelle Kennedy, who portrayed baby Elizabeth. Production quickly resumed, thanks to the efforts of prop master Wagner, who, as luck would have it, has a background in child psychology and a special way with kids.

Wagner continues to work closely with the twins as they reprise their role in the NBC-TV comedy series "Baby Boom," based on the film. The series, premiering Wednesday, November 2 (9:30–10:00 P.M. NYT; in stereo; closed-captioned), stars Kate Jackson as J. C. Wiatt, a single mother trying to juggle a high-powered career and motherhood.

Wagner is officially credited as the "baby wrangler," but an early improvisation earned him the lasting nickname of "Bubbles."

"My main avocation has become wandering through toy stores looking for unusual things," confesses Wagner. "I use toys to get the babies' attention and elicit certain reactions that fit the scene. For example, I have five different kinds of flashlights, which are helpful in getting the kids to follow camera eye lines."

According to Wagner, the biggest challenge in working with babies is that scripts often call for them to do or say something that is beyond their normal stage of development. "At age three, kids generally don't speak in complete sentences, and their elocution can be far from comprehensible," he says. "I think I do what all good directors do. I pull talent and performances out of the kids that they didn't know or didn't think they had in them. It's very rewarding and gratifying work."

Wagner's special camaraderie with the Kennedy children reflects his years as a child psychologist. A Chicago native, Wagner earned a master's degree in child development from Loyola University and later worked with juvenile delinquents and autistic children in Chicago.

He often uses various animal imitations to draw out dramatic performances from Kristina and Michelle. "We've discovered that lizards look scared with their big bulging eyes; giraffes look sad with their huge pouting lips; and turkeys can look silly with their little flashing eyes. By the end of shooting this season's episodes, I'm sure we will have gone through the whole zoo!"

Media Rep: Jane Doe, Series Programs, (202) 555–1234, NBC—New York
[Date code]

Following is a news release, prepared by Bob Meyer for doctoral candidate, Peter Graves, aimed at the consumer press, with a direct lead soliciting volunteers for his study:

FOR IMMEDIATE RELEASE   Contact: John Doe
[Month, date, year]   (202) 555–1234

SUBJECTS SOUGHT FOR STUDY OF UNIQUE ISSUES
FACING PARTNERS OF PWAs

$50 Paid to Each Volunteer

Volunteers will receive $50 for participating in a study designed to help understand the needs and experiences of partners of Persons with Aids (PWAs).

The $50 honorarium (paid directly to the volunteer or to the charity of their choice) is available to subjects who are a partner of a person with AIDS, who does not have AIDS himself (but may have tested HIV+) and who had been in a relationship with the PWA prior to the diagnosis. Participating in the study involves being interviewed twice at times and places most convenient to them. All information is coded to insure strict confidentiality.

Supported in part by a grant from the Los Angeles Society of Clinical Psychologists and approved by the University of Illinois at Chicago, the study is being conducted be Peter K. Graves, a gay candidate for a Ph.D. in psychology and a member of the psychology staff of a large Los Angeles medical facility.

"It is imperative that we reduce the stigma and misinformation which are the greatest barriers to prevention and effective treatment of this decade-old epidemic," says Graves, who developed this study while facilitating a therapy group for significant others of PWAs in Chicago.

"I hope to learn more about the support that is or is not available from family and friends, plus public and private organizations, in addition to how PWA's partners feel about it," adds Graves.

Potential subjects can contact Graves via a "no obligation" phone call to (202) 555-1234. If you get the answering machine, either leave a message indicating how to contact you, or, if you prefer, call back between 5:00 and 9:00 most evenings or anytime on weekends.

The study is planned to be completed by fall 1993, and interested participants will be given study results, as well as any resources or other materials Graves can provide.

Quotations

Quotations are used to lend personal authority to a statement your client wishes to make. They are a standard element in public relations writing, particularly news releases. When drafting a news release on a new product, for example, you must often invent a comment from a product manager on the feature of a new product or perhaps on its application in the marketplace. Your made-up quotation will invariably have to be approved by that person. Even if your quotation is taken verbatim from its source, however, it should be approved by that source before it is released.

Journalists quote people directly, and any modifications the journalists make to these quotations are noted with brackets or other explanations. In public relations writing, however, because you are often called on to make up quotations, bear in mind that the substance and tone of the quotation should be in keeping with the needs of your client. For example, here is a quotation appropriate to its source:

> Research and Development Director Doe said of the Magna 260 tank, "The proven kill ratio of the Magna 260 exceeds that of the existing Tiger 9 by two to one, in effect enabling our nation to double its defense capabilities."

Quotations should provide only relevant information. As a public relations practitioner, you must remain keenly aware of the interests of your audience and your client; don't clutter a news release with unneeded facts.

Photos, Samples, and Review Copies

Whenever appropriate, you should state that a photo or color slide, a sample, or a review copy of the subject of the release is available on request (if it is not already enclosed with the release). Jim Feldman, a music critic for the *Village Voice,* says publicists frequently call to ask if he's received their releases about a new rock band, and whether he wants to interview the band members. If the music critic has never heard the band, has no idea of what they sound like, and has not received a compact disc or been invited to hear the band perform, there is no chance the reporter will *know* if he has an interest in writing about it, let alone whether he wants to do an interview.

Make it as easy as possible for the journalist to experience first-hand the subject of your press release. If the release is about a speech, attach a complete text of that speech. If the release is about a new fabric, attach a swatch. When a sample cannot be enclosed, invite the reporter to a place where the subject of the news release can be viewed or encountered.

Style and Form

A consistent style and format give your news release a professional look. There are a number of guides or stylebooks on the market. Since you are most often sending your release to newsrooms, however, we recommend the *AP Stylebook,* which is used in most newsrooms across the country.

All news releases must have these four key elements:

1. *Date and embargo.* Include a date indicating when the release is issued and another date indicating when it should be made public. Any restriction on when the information may be used is called an embargo. An embargo is usually used when issuing information that can be released to the public only after a specified date and time. Embargoes can be tricky, and should be used cautiously. If one member of the press ignores the embargo and breaks the story early, others will probably do the same. If your release has no time restrictions for going public, it is marked "For Immediate Release."

2. *Contact.* Include the name and phone number of the person to whom inquiries should be directed. For breaking stories of great urgency, you may want to include a home phone number if information will be needed by the media during non–office hours.

3. *Headline.* Include a headline at the top of the release to summarize the story and catch the reader's attention. When the story is complicated, use a subhead as well. Headline information is drawn from the body of the release, because the release must hold up as a complete thought without the headline. Headlines are important, even though editors almost always write their own. For one thing, they help direct an editor's view of your subject. For another, they are your "advertisement," since, based on your headline, editors decide whether or not to keep reading.

4. *Letterhead.* Use the official letterhead of your company or the client you're representing. The letterhead lends credibility and professionalism to your presentation, and it often includes useful information, such as the fax number and address.

These elements can be arranged several ways in a news release. Here are two examples of the most typical and accepted styles:

a. *Block Style*

Contact: John Doe	Month, date, year
(202) 555–1234	For Immediate Release

HEADLINE GOES HERE

Use Subheads When Stories Are Complicated

The text of the release begins here. . . .

b. *Newspaper Style*

For Immediate Release

HEADLINE GOES HERE

Use Subheads When Stories Are Complicated

[CITY, month, date]—The text of the release starts here, in paragraph form. . . .

When you use this latter form, insert a six-digit code at the end of the release to indicate the full date. For example, the code for May 29, 1993, would be 052993.

Some press releases carry the date and embargo on the top and list the contact and phone number at the bottom. Each public relations office has its own style for laying out the essential elements of a press release. What is important is that all four elements—date and embargo, contact, headline, and letterhead—are included and easy to find.

Here are some additional points of style that should be followed in formatting press releases:

- All copy should be typewritten and double-spaced on a single side of standard 8½-by-11-inch paper.
- Reasonable margins of at least an inch should appear on all sides of the paper.
- When the press release continues for more than a page, include the word *more* or *continued* at the bottom of the page to lead readers onward.
- Short paragraphs are best. Don't be afraid to use one-sentence paragraphs.
- Most publications use capitalization sparingly, and you should too, within the limits of your company's or client's style. Given the choice, make titles such as vice-president and chief

executive officer lowercase. Here's a common rule of thumb to follow: When a *title* is given, capitalize it (e.g., John Doe, Senior Director, Sales), but when a *position* is given, use lowercase (e.g., John Doe is the senior director of the sales department).

• Consistency of style is very important. If your company or client has a style sheet, use it.

The Q&A

If your release presents a complicated story, you may find it useful to attach a question-and-answer sheet (Q&A) that anticipates questions reporters will have. Sometimes such a sheet is helpful to have for your own internal use in responding to inquiries from the press.

Here is an example of questions and answers compiled by the Nestle Carnation Food Company in connection with the introduction of its Good Start infant formula:

IRON IN THE FIRST YEAR OF LIFE: DR. LILLIAN BEARD RESPONDS

Why is iron important for babies?

Beard: The first year of life is a crucial time in a baby's development. During that first year of life, the baby's birth weight triples and the brain size doubles. To accommodate this growth, infants are born with a store of iron which can sustain their needs for the first four to six months of life. After this period, they need one to two times the dietary iron of a full-grown male.

How common is iron deficiency?

Beard: Iron deficiency problems are more widespread than many parents might suspect. One study found that 27.3 percent of nine- to 12-month-old infants had iron deficiency without anemia.

In addition, this Q&A offered short but detailed answers to the following questions:

What happens if a baby doesn't get enough iron?
If babies are starting to eat iron-fortified cereal, won't that provide sufficient iron?

Are there any specific factors that can put babies at risk for iron deficiency?

Here is another example of a Q&A used by Intersource in the introduction of a new light bulb:

THE E-LAMP BACKGROUND

Most Frequently Asked Questions about the E-Lamp

This background paper deals with many of the frequently asked questions Intersource has received from around the world. Additional information is available from Intersource Technologies Corporate Relations Office.

- *Will the E-Lamp interfere with TV, radio or appliances?*
  No, the E-Lamp has been tested and approved to standards set by the Federal Communications Commission for all electronic devices (FCC Part 15 and Part 18). Even large numbers of E-Lamps can be used in residential or commercial settings with no interference.

The following questions were also answered in this extensive Q&A:

- *How does the E-Lamp differ from the compact fluorescent on the market?*
- *How does the E-Lamp differ from other "long-life" bulbs on the market?*
- *Are there any health or environmental hazards for the E-Lamp?*
- *How much will the E-Lamp cost?*
- *Why would someone pay $20 for a light bulb?*
- *Who will build the E-Lamp?*
- *Who will sell the E-Lamp?*
- *General Electric claims they had one of these in the '70s. Why do you claim it is new now when it has been around for so long?*
- *Who actually developed the E-Lamp?*
- *Is the bulb patented?*
- *Why are the electric utility companies interested in saving power?*
- *We don't have an energy shortage now. Why all the fuss?*
- *Why would consumer and ecology groups endorse this bulb?*
- *Where can the E-Lamp be used?*

- *Please describe the general features of the E-Lamp.*
- *When will the product be available?*

Photo Captions

Photographs are an important way to document and publicize your subject. Many publications will run photos supplied by public relations offices if the photos meet certain standards of professional quality. Whenever possible, you should hire your own photographer. The usual format to send is an 8-by-10-inch black-and-white enlargement. If the subject of the photo is a candidate for a magazine cover story, or if you are aiming for placements in magazine stories or in newspapers that use color art in certain sections, you should also supply reproduction-quality color slides, or indicate that color art is available on request.

If you send an interesting, high-quality 8-by-10 photograph with your news release, there is a good chance the editor will decide to run it with the story, giving your story bigger play. At most publications, it is rare that an editor will assign a staff photographer to shoot photographs to accompany a story generated by a press release.

Because readers are more likely to look at photos than read a text, you, as a public relations representative, should always be considering newsworthy photo opportunities that tell a story. Dignitaries, celebrities and public officials are usually considered newsworthy by the trade and consumer press. Photos of senior management such as presidents and key executive officers are often considered newsworthy by the trade press.

Except for product photos, which are primarily static shots, photos featuring subjects in action are always more interesting than posed shots. When people are to be featured in photos, try to have them *doing* something rather than staring into the camera. At photo sessions or during events, encourage people being photographed to be naturally active, depending on the situation. Avoid simple head shots, except for photos that accompany appointment releases.

The subjects in photos should always be identified and described in a caption when the photos are sent out. A photo caption, also called a cutline, is best written in the present tense and active voice. Choose one verb that best explains the action and circumstance in the photo and state the basic five W's surrounding the picture:

- Who
- What
- Where
- When
- Why

Headlines for Photo Captions

Photo captions that are stand-alone art—meaning they do not accompany a story—usually carry a headline. For example, shown in Figures 1 and 2 are photo captions from the *New York Times* that are complete stories and use headlines.

Reuters

The Party's Over as Fat Tuesday Sings With Merriment

Floats from the Krewe of Rex passing yesterday through downtown New Orleans. Mardi Gras, French for "fat Tuesday," culminated the carnival season in South Louisiana that began with Twelfth Night, Jan. 6, and ends at the start of Ash Wednesday at midnight, the beginning of Lent.

FIGURE 1

Advocates for Animal Rights Protest Transplants

Robert Winter, right, who says he has liver disease, confronts Lynn Wagner, an animal-rights advocate, during a protest in Pittsburgh against the transplanting of animal organs into humans. The group protested outside the home of Dr. Thomas Starzi, a surgeon involved in transplants. The nation's second person to receive a baboon liver died Friday from an abdominal infection.

FIGURE 2

When a photo is used to accompany a story, a headline is not necessary.

Groups of people shown in photos are usually identified in order from left to right, this way:

Pictured from left are board members being sworn in: (bottom row) John Smith, Bill Anderson, Charlotte Brown, and Jim Brown; (top row) Joyce Barlow, Edna Goodman, and Ellen Simpson.

If the names in a photo caption need titles as well, use semicolons to separate the subjects in the list:

Pictured from left are board members being sworn in: (bottom row) John Smith, vice-president, marketing; Bill Anderson, treasurer; Charlotte Brown, public relations director.

Cutlines (captions) can be attached to photos with a paperclip in the corner (if the clip will not damage the photo) or with a small piece of tape that easily peels off, with the copy curling around the bottom of the page, as in Figure 3.

A photo caption can also be printed on the bottom of the photo, as shown in Figure 4.

Do not use a permanent label to attach a caption to the back of a photo. An editor should be able to remove the caption and edit it on paper.

When sending out photos, make sure they are properly packaged

PICTURED: Elizabeth Taylor, Johnny Carson

Johnny Carson welcomed superstar Elizabeth Taylor on her first visit to "The Tonight Show" — her first late-night television talk show appearance — February 21, 1992.

FIGURE 3

SELA WARD stars
as Teddy Reed.

FIGURE 4

with cardboard or are put into inflexible envelopes to avoid damage, and mark or stamp the package "Photos—Do Not Bend."

Most publications use black-and-white shots. Your photographer should give you contact sheets, from which you can then choose the shots you want printed.

Media Kits

A media kit, also referred to as a press kit, is an organized, comprehensive package of information on your client. Media kits are often compilations of several of the kinds of public relations writing discussed above.

Items in a media kit vary, depending on the client, but standard contents may include hard news releases and feature news releases; a Q&A; biographies and backgrounders (discussed in Chapter 3); photos of the key executives and/or products; and lists of goods manufactured, achievements or honors received, or films or records released. Sometimes media kits include annual reports, brochures, or publications, such as those discussed in Chapter 8.

Photocopies of other articles already published about the client can be particularly useful in press kits. They can influence editors to do stories, while at the same time avoiding duplication. Make sure such copies always include the date they originally appeared and where they were published.

A media kit helps a journalist by making background information readily available, thereby saving research time. Public relations offices get very busy, and you won't always have time to compile a kit every time you need one. Prepare them in advance so that you can send them at a moment's notice.

Media kits are also frequently put together for a special event. If, for example, you're holding a media conference to announce award recipients, the media kit will most likely include short biographies of the award recipients, background on the awards and their sponsor, and, when applicable, samples of what warranted the award (perhaps photographs, artwork, essays, etc.).

Sometimes media kits are compiled in response to breaking stories. In those situations, they may contain reports, court records, and other documents that support or refute a claim.

Media kits are often packaged in custom-printed folders with the client's logo on them. This presentation is attractive but not mandatory. A less expensive kit can be packaged in a glossy colored pocket folder available as a standard office supply.

Here are the elements that Hill & Knowlton included in the media kit announcing the new line of juices:

- A press release on the new product.
- A fact sheet on the juices, with information on flavors, packaging, storage, availability, cost, and the manufacturer (including its name and address).
- A background piece titled "Welch Foods through the Years," which described milestones in the company's growth since its formation in 1853.
- A feature release on the importance of the morning meal, according to nutritionists, and how the new juices could provide a quick, easy, healthful breakfast.
- Two product photos, one picturing juice cans surrounded by their fruit sources and the other showing a breakfast shake in a glass beside a blender.

The media kit announcing the new E-Lamp included the following elements:

- A Q&A on the most frequently asked questions about the E-Lamp.
- A background story on the history of lighting.
- An explanation, both in prose and in diagrams, of the E-Lamp technology.
- Copies of the text the senior officials delivered.
- A corporate backgrounder on Intersource Technologies and biographies of the administrative and technical staff members.
- Copies of newspaper stories that ran on the subject.

Approvals

To prevent misstatements of fact or divulgence of inappropriate information, a series of approvals is necessary before a news release—or public relations material of any sort—is sent to the media. The line of copy approval can be quite long, and several rounds of rewrites and approvals are frequently needed before copy can be released. Be accommodating and rewrite according to suggestions and comments from those approving copy. If you disagree with a change that makes a substantive difference, tactfully and succinctly explain your point of view. Perhaps you can suggest an alternative phrasing that both of you are comfortable with.

In a corporation, there is likely to be a series of people in management who must read and approve your copy before it can be released. In most companies, a high-ranking member of the legal department is part of the review process. Because anything released to the media becomes part of the company's public image, the approval process often goes to the top of the corporate structure.

In an agency, your copy is usually first approved by your supervisor and then sent to your client, where it must go through the company's established approval process before it can be sent to the media.

Because of the labyrinth of approvals through which a document must travel, it's a good idea to ask for dated initials on approved copy. This will help avoid confusion later as to who saw what when. Don't be insulted or discouraged when your copy is altered. It doesn't necessarily mean that you haven't done a good writing job. There is simply a lot of rewriting that has to be done in public relations, and clients often have specific ideas they would like to see communicated through your writing.

There may be times when you feel your client is making copy changes that will not advance his or her goals or communicate them as clearly as you would wish. You must be the judge of when and whether you should point them out. Your dual role is to serve your clients' needs as well as the needs of the target audience.

Our Main Point: Never send a news release to the media *before* it goes through all necessary approval stages.

Chapter Recap

The most important guidelines to keep in mind while researching and writing a news release are as follows:

1. Make sure your subject is newsworthy.
2. Make sure the release will advance your client's objectives.
3. Summarize the entire story in the first paragraph. Or, if it is

a feature, make sure the first paragraph will capture and
hold the reader's interest.

4. Write it in the pyramid news style.
5. Answer all the logical questions the release is likely to raise.
6. Attribute the announcement to an official source.
7. Check all information for accuracy.
8. Include a date and embargo (the date the news may be
   released), contact and phone number, and headline.
9. Provide copy that is typewritten and double-spaced, with
   adequate margins.
10. Release it only after you have obtained all the necessary
    approvals.

2

The Pitch Letter

Keeping Your Story out of the Circular File

The goal of most public relations work is to gain media interest in your story. The first step toward media coverage is usually a letter that introduces your story idea. Such a letter is commonly referred to as a pitch letter.

The pitch letter often determines whether an editor or reporter pursues a story. Because most editors and reporters are extremely busy and don't have much time for phone calls, they often prefer to receive pitches and background material by mail. A letter saves time, can be read at the person's convenience, and is a polite, unobtrusive way to present your ideas.

Pitch letters are used for all kinds of reasons: as cover letters attached to press releases, as invitations to events, as requests for endorsements or contributions, and so on. Not all pitch letters come from public relations offices. Television newswoman Barbara Walters, for example, once remarked that when she's soliciting an interview, she starts by sending a letter. Still, the most typical pitch letter is sent by a public relations representative to inspire a reporter to cover a story.

In addition to suggesting a newsworthy story idea, good pitch letters offer substantive background information, help set up interviews and, when appropriate, accompany samples of products you may be pitching.

In short, not only do you suggest a good story idea, but you also make it easy for the reporter to cover the story in depth.

Form and Tone

Pitch letters should always be typewritten neatly in standard business-letter form on official letterhead. The following is an example of a proper business letter:

Date

Mr. John Doe
123 Main Street
Anytown, MO 63110

Dear Mr. Doe:

As you know, letter writing is an important part of business communications in general, and of public relations in particular.

Using stationery with an official letterhead is always recommended. It reflects seriousness and professionalism.

You should also be aware that there are standard spacings in a business letter: four spaces between date and addressee; two spaces between salutation and first paragraph; two spaces between paragraphs; and four spaces for the signature between sign-off and the author's name.

This letter is written in a flush-left, block-style form. There are other options, such as putting the date on the right-hand side and indenting all paragraphs. What is important is that you choose one style and follow it consistently.

Thank you for your attention to this matter.

Sincerely,

Jane Doe
Account Executive

The letter reflects your—and your client's—level of professionalism and competence. Grammar and punctuation should be perfect. If your letter is sloppy, an editor might infer that your information is too, and might also discount your ideas.

Unless you are friendly with the person to whom you are writing, do not use a highly personal tone, and certainly do not address him or her by first name. On the other hand, don't make the letter too stuffy or formal either. Most of the time, you will be writing to editors and reporters you don't know, or don't know well. Be professional and polite in your approach, and you won't go wrong.

The following is an example of a pitch letter about a development in TV technology.

Date

Mr. Bob Smith
Editor
Video Talk
111 Elm Avenue
Anytown, MO 63110

Dear Mr. Smith:

At the recent Japan Electronics Show in Tokyo, five of the eight largest Japanese electronics firms featured "New Media" as their main exhibition. New Media has taken Japan by storm, and it is only a matter of time before it hits the United States.

What is New Media and why are Japanese companies so excited about it? Kobe Electric, a major manufacturer of consumer electronics products, has put together a brief background paper on New Media and its expected impact on the consumer electronics market.

Attached is a copy of the paper; I hope you find it interesting and useful. If you have any questions, please call me at (202) 555-1234.

Thank you for your interest in Kobe Electric.

Sincerely,

John Doe
Account Executive

This next one sets up an interview:

Date

Mr. Don Smith
Editor
Watch Talk
44 East Street
New York, NY 10000

Dear Mr. Smith:

Thanks for giving me a few minutes to speak to you yesterday about some ideas for a story on wristwatch technology.

As I mentioned, I think "The Creation of a Watch" might be a good idea. I'd like to offer you an opportunity to visit Macho Watches in Rolly, New Jersey, and discuss with engineers, designers, and marketing people just exactly how a watch is created—from beginning to end.

We can take you step by step to talk with people behind the scenes in:

- Research and development
- Product engineering
- Design
- Mass marketing

I should mention that Macho is one of the few companies that produces wristwatches in America—right in Rolly, New Jersey!

I'll give you a call soon to see if we can arrange a visit for you.

Thanks for your interest.

Sincerely,

John Doe
Account Executive

And this one attempts to inspire interest in the results of a survey:

Date

Ms. Ann Smith
Office Talk
11 Bark Avenue
Townville, CA 90003

Dear Ms. Smith:

As we discussed, I'm sending along information on the latest King Steno survey of office personnel.

Among the findings in the survey:

- More than 93 percent of secretaries surveyed say they are happy in their careers—but very few want their children to follow in their footsteps.

- Almost 90 percent regard computer skills as a vehicle for moving up into management ranks. Despite this optimism, only 30 percent see themselves achieving that promotion.
- Although many people have predicted that office automation would cut secretarial jobs, more than 50 percent of secretaries surveyed felt automation has improved their relationships with their bosses.

The survey also provides surprising revelations about secretarial attitudes toward new technology, the effect of computers on interoffice relationships, and predictions about the impact computers will have on the secretarial job market in the future.

After you've had a chance to look over the study, I'll give you a call to see if you need any further information.

Cordially,

John Doe
Account Executive

What Makes a Good Pitch Letter

Notice the common elements in all of these pitch letters: They're short (no longer than one page), to the point, catchy, and full of information. Reporters are inundated with public relations material every day. Pitch letters, therefore, must get to the right person, get to the point, intrigue the reader, and contain substantive information.

The process for presenting a good pitch can be broken down into five stages:

1. Analyze the subject and identify the target.
2. Call the editor.
3. Write a catchy lead.
4. Compose brief, informative text.
5. Wrap it up.

Analyze the Subject and Identify the Target

The key to a good pitch letter is the "hook," or news angle, it offers. To find that hook, you must first understand the subject you're pitching and then consider the needs of the journalist who will receive the pitch letter.

If you're trying to promote a story about a videotape recorder, the first step is to understand all you can about that recorder and what makes it newsworthy and different from all others. Most of this information will be readily available to you, but if it's not, seek it out. This may mean phone calls to engineers who designed the product or to salespeople who understand its position in the marketplace. And most importantly, you must know how your client or your boss wants the product presented to the press.

Once you understand why your product is special, you then turn your attention to your target media. If, for example, you want the trade magazine *Videography* to write about this videotape recorder, your approach should be technical and indepth. If, however, you want *USA Today,* a consumer newspaper, to write about it, your approach will be entirely different, geared more toward general information.

Assuming *Videography* is the target of your first pitch letter, you must find out who specifically at the magazine would write an article about the product you are pitching, and you must know what types of articles are published in *Videography.* Get some back issues of the magazine and look at the tables of contents.

By looking at the table of contents, you'll see that there are regular departments, such as "Latebreak," "Marketing: Hardware," and "Production." In addition, there are several feature articles in each issue, along with a number of regular columns. After carefully studying three or four issues of the magazine and analyzing the product you're pitching, you should now be ready to start developing a pitch letter that is suited to *Videography.*

Call the Editor

Now that you're familiar with both the subject you are pitching and the target of your pitch, your next step is to call the editor. In some cases, you will know who the editor is, but most often, you won't. Call the publication and ask who covers stories on videotape-recorder technology.

Once you know whom you should call, you can make a brief pitch over the phone. Some editors will have time to talk and will encourage you to elaborate on your ideas. Many, however, will tell you to mail information to them so they can look it over. Their time on the phone is limited, so get to the point quickly and be brief. Having notes in front of you will help.

Introduce yourself using your first and last name, and explain why you are calling. For example, "My name is John Smith, I'm calling from XYZ Public Relations, and I represent General Electronics." Explain that you have information on a new videotape recorder that plays in reverse and has stereo sound, and that you think it would be a good story for a "New Products" column. The editor may tell you it sounds interesting and request your material, or he or she may direct you to someone else on the staff.

If an editor rejects your story immediately, listen carefully to the reasons (if they are offered). You can learn what will be better suited to that editor's needs the next time. Simply say "thank you" and get on to your next call. When the editor encourages you to send more information, confirm the spelling of the editor's name and the accuracy of the address. (You may want to make a separate call to ask the receptionist to confirm these.) Your credibility will be hard to establish if you get them wrong!

You now have the right name and address and the right angle of approach.

Tip: If an editor consistently receives good ideas and timely, useful information from you, he or she will begin to give your correspondence more attention. On the other hand, if an editor frequently receives inappropriate letters and releases from you, most of your material will end up in the garbage can, possibly unopened.

Write a Catchy Lead

The opening paragraph of a pitch letter should be a good one, because it's the best chance you have to interest an editor. William Ruder, a founder of the public relations agency Ruder Finn, says that in all types of pitch letters, "You're dead or alive after the first sentence."

As in all good copy, the lead of a pitch letter should be enticing and informative; it should make the editor want to read on. Here are some good opening paragraphs:

Ms. Jane Doe
The Living Arts
New York Times
229 West 43rd St.
New York, NY 10036

Dear Ms. Doe:

Did you know that while 93 percent of today's secretaries say they are happy in their careers, very few of them want their children to follow in their footsteps?

Ms. Jane Doe
Advertising Age
220 East 42nd St.
New York, NY 10017

Dear Ms. Doe:

As you know, prerecorded video was a red-hot industry this past year, with some 230 million prerecorded cassettes being shipped. Most industry watchers predict that figure will double by the year 2000.

Ms. Jane Doe
Senior Editor
Computerworld
375 Cochituate Road
Framingham, MA 01701

Dear Ms. Doe:

General Electric Information Services Company, a major supplier of computing services, has just completed the world's largest commercially available teleprocessing network. Its three computer centers carry the processing load for more than 6,000 customers worldwide.

Ms. Jane Doe
"48 Hours"
CBS Television Network
51 West 52nd Street
New York, NY 10019

Dear Ms. Doe:

Just outside the city limits of Knoxville, Tennessee, 110 blue-collar American laborers are working their hearts out for a $50 billion Japanese conglomerate, and loving it.

A common element can be seen in these opening paragraphs. Each one focuses on a subject that could interest the editor addressed. Each one also contains impressive facts and figures, and each one is intriguing to someone who covers those particular fields.

The first sentence is often the hardest part of a pitch letter to write. One of the best ways to formulate an opening line is to single out the most newsworthy aspect of the subject you are pitching and state it simply. If, for example, you are pitching a story on the world's first talking computer for IBM, your opening sentence could very well be "IBM has developed the world's first talking computer."

If, however, you are pitching a case history, an interview, or a survey, you need to build up to the pitch with a provocative opening. The letter to the *New York Times* is a good example of this type of opening line: "Did you know that while 93 percent of today's secretaries . . . " It's a catchy opening, urging the editor to read on and find out where this fact came from and where it is leading. That letter was sent to pitch a story on the results of a survey taken by Kelly Services on the automated office. It's an example of how to make a dry subject interesting.

When writing an opening line, try to come up with something fresh and intriguing. Don't use the first paragraph to give a lengthy history of the company you are pitching, or to explain who you are and what your job is. And don't tell the editor about his or her readership. Many novice writers make the mistake of opening a pitch letter with something like "The readers of *Videography* are interested in the latest developments in the video industry." That sentence only reiterates the obvious. Certainly a reporter for *Videography* will know what the magazine's readers are interested in; don't waste time by pointing that out.

Compose Brief, Informative Text

Once the opening paragraph has caught your reader's attention, the rest of the letter must flow smoothly and logically. If your opening line is "IBM has developed the world's first talking computer," then your next sentence should take a natural step in backing up or expanding on that claim.

Thus, the second sentence might well be this: "The effect of such a development may permanently change the way Americans work, according to Mr. John Doe, Vice-President of Product Research for IBM. Mr. Doe contends that a talking computer will . . . ," and so on. Stick to the facts and avoid using adjectives, especially words like *unique, greatest, phenomenal,* and *incredible,* which are overused and rarely true.

If you look back at the sample pitch letters in the beginning of this chapter, you will see that they all flow smoothly and head toward an ultimate purpose, whether it be for the editor to read a product description, tour a watch factory, or study a survey.

The middle section of a pitch letter is often where the story information, or "meat," is found. This is where you expand on the central idea. It is here that you explain how Kelly Services has taken a survey of 2,000 secretaries throughout the nation, how General Electric Information Services is upgrading three of its computer centers at a cost of $60 million, or what five principles Matsushita Electric is using to manage American employees at its factory in Tennessee.

When you have several crucial points of information to get across, it is often helpful to list them in "bullet" form—that is, to indent and set them off with a bullet or some other typographic device. For example, let's look again at the pitch letter trying to interest an editor in doing a story on Macho watches. After an opening hook, the author gets down to the real purpose of the letter in the second and third paragraphs and uses bullets to save time and space.

Date

Mr. Don Smith
Editor
Watch Talk
44 East Street
New York, NY 10000

Dear Mr. Smith:

Thanks for giving me a few minutes to speak to you yesterday about some ideas for a story on wristwatch technology.

As I mentioned, I think "The Creation of a Watch" might be a good idea. I'd like to offer you an opportunity to visit Macho Watches in Rolly, New Jersey, and discuss with engineers, designers, and marketing people just exactly how a watch is created—from beginning to end.

We can take you step by step to talk with people behind the scenes in:

- Research and development
- Product engineering
- Design
- Mass marketing

I should mention that Macho is one of the few companies that produces wristwatches in America—right in Rolly, New Jersey!

I'll give you a call soon to see if we can arrange a visit for you.

Thanks for your interest. I hope we can work together on this project.

Sincerely,

John Doe
Account Executive

The bullet technique is quite effective, because it allows editors to quickly see what kind of information you're offering.

Here's an example from a pitch letter accompanying a press kit on TV technology:

Enclosed you will find information on the following products:

- World's smallest color TV
- World's first hand-held TV
- A forty-foot video screen for stadiums
- A 3-D TV system for home viewing

Through use of techniques like the bullet method, you can pack in a great deal of hard facts, clearly and concisely.

Whether you use bullets or straight prose, always keep your letter short. Rarely are you justified in writing a pitch letter longer than one page. When you have finished a draft, ask yourself a few questions:

1. *Is there any redundancy in the letter?* Redundant phrases plague business correspondence. There is no room for saying things twice in any type of public relations writing. For example, do

away with phrases like "Seventy-five *different* countries"; saying "seventy-five countries" is enough. Similarly, phrases such as "unique and different," "new and innovative," or "at the forefront of the cutting edge" are all redundant.

2. *Is there any information that is not vital to the story?* When you are developing a pitch letter, it's easy to include information that is not germane. Reread the letter carefully to make sure everything you've written is absolutely central to the pitch. Eliminate excess.

3. *Is there a faster way to get to the point?* Don't waste time leading up to the subject of a pitch letter. By the third paragraph, the editor had better know why you've sent the letter. Make sure you're not beating around the bush.

Wrap it Up

There are standard lines for ending pitch letters. Writers each have their own preference, but most end their letters with sentences like these:

> "After you've had a chance to review the material, I'll call to see if you're interested in pursuing a story."
>
> *or*
>
> "If you'd like any further information on this subject; please call me at (202) 555–1234."
>
> *or*
>
> "I'll give you a call early next week to see if you're interested."
>
> *or*
>
> "Thank you for your time and consideration."

It is best to follow up a pitch letter with a phone call to see if the reporter received the material and has any interest in the story. But remember that reporters are extremely busy and may not have time even to take your call.

Use discretion to identify whom to call and when. For example, editors on morning newspapers are on deadline in the afternoon, so the best times to call them are usually between 10:00 A.M. and noon. Radio and television editors have varying deadlines, but one rule is safe: Never call right before their airtime.

As we've shown, the pitch letter is crucial to effective public relations. Take the time to prepare it correctly.

Chapter Recap

In review, here are the steps for successful pitch letters:

1. Analyze the subject and identify the target.
2. Call the editor.
3. Write a catchy lead.
4. Compose brief, informative text.
5. Wrap it up.

3

The Biography and Backgrounder

Bringing Your Subject to Life

Public relations biographies follow two forms. One is the newspaper-style résumé that offers background information in a simple and comprehensive way. The other is a feature biography that is more like a magazine story or personality profile on the subject.

Whereas biographies, often referred to as bios, are written on people, backgrounders, while similar in form to biographies, are written on companies, products, and places. And obituaries, frequently called obits, are essentially bios, with the lead offering details about the person's date and cause of death.

Biographies and backgrounders are often accompanied by fact sheets that simplify complicated information by breaking it down into various categories. Histories of events, products, or companies are often presented in time lines, which are chronological lists of information.

This chapter discusses the creation and construction of news and feature bios, obits, backgrounders, fact sheets, and time lines.

Biographies

The ten essential steps to writing an effective bio are as follows:

1. Work from a sensibly constructed outline.
2. Command authority with the lead.
3. Clarify, simplify, and condense.
4. Vary language and sentence structure.
5. Connect thoughts.

6. Attribute quotations.
7. Back up all your claims.
8. Use one tense.
9. Assume nothing on the part of the reader.
10. Proofread carefully.

These steps will be discussed in detail, but first let's examine the construction of bios.

The structure of biographies is similar to that of appointment releases, discussed in Chapter 1. Although the content of each bio will differ, of course, depending on the person it is written about, the framework for all bios does not vary much and generally conforms to the following outline:

• Opens by identifying the subject by name, title, and other relevant attributes
• Summarizes the scope of the person's activities
• Offers educational and professional background on the person
• Saves personal information for the end, if such data is to be included at all

Here is an example of how easily an appointment release (see Chapter 1, p. 6) becomes a newspaper-style bio with a minor adjustment to the lead:

BIO: DR. NICHOLAS H. ADDAMS

Dr. Nicholas H. Addams, Vice President of Product Development for ABC Electric, is responsible for approving and supervising the design and production of all products developed by ABC Electric for consumer and industrial use.

Previously, Addams had been the director of Consumer Products Development since June 1987. In that position, he coordinated the development of various electronic home conveniences—including breakthrough voice-activated home heating and lighting systems—as well as ABC Electric's tremendously successful home security systems, invisible fences, and audiovisual home entertainment centers.

Before that, from February 1982 until May 1987, Addams was a special-projects director for ABC Electric's international trade and consumer expositions.

Addams came to ABC Electric from the New York industrial electronics company Omega Development, Inc., where he had been a design manager in the factory equipment division from January 1980 until January 1982. While serving in that role, he also became involved in the marketing end of the industry, by working as a technical planner, adviser, and lecturer at Omega's semiannual trade shows. From October 1978 until December 1980, he was the engineering manager in the robotics department, where he had started with the company as an engineer in February 1976.

A 1975 graduate of the Massachusetts Institute of Technology with a doctorate in mechanical engineering, Addams earlier received an M.S. degree in computer science (1971) and a B.S. degree in physics (1969) from Rensselaer Polytechnic Institute in his native Troy, New York.

Addams lives in Fort Lee, New Jersey, with his wife, Hillary.

CONTACT: John Doe, ABC Electric Publicity, (202) 555–1234
ABC Electric, [month, date, year]

Here is an example of another newspaper-style bio of a vice-president at NBC:

BETTY HUDSON

Senior Vice-President, Corporate Communications
National Broadcasting Company

Betty Hudson became Senior Vice-President, Corporate Communications, NBC, in March 1989. She supervises all of NBC's East and West Coast Corporate Communications activities, including NBC Media Relations, NBC Corporate Communications, NBC Employee Communications, NBC Talent and Media Services (which includes NBC Guest Relations), NBC Editorial Services, and NBC Corporate Events and Travel Services.

Hudson had been Vice-President, Corporate and Media Relations, NBC, since July 1986. She assumed responsibility for NBC Corporate Communications in May 1988.

She joined NBC in February 1979 as Vice-President, Corporate Projects, and was named Vice-President, Corporate Relations and Advertising, in October 1984.

A native of Atlanta, Georgia, Hudson began her career as an advertising copywriter and on-air talent at WCBD-TV in Charleston,

South Carolina. She subsequently served as director of promotion for three NBC-TV affiliates: WCIV-TV, Charleston; WAVE-TV, Louisville, Kentucky; and WSB-TV, Atlanta.

She earned a degree in advertising and public relations from the University of Georgia.

Hudson was named Outstanding Young Careerist by the South Carolina Business and Professional Women's Association in 1976 and received the John E. Dewey Award from the University of Georgia in 1984. She served the university as a member of its Bicentennial Committee and as a regional vice-president of its alumna society. In January 1986, she was awarded an honorary Doctorate of Commercial Science by St. John's University in New York. She is past President of the International Radio and Television Society and serves on the boards of the American Women in Radio and Television Foundation, KIDSNET, and the Broadcast Education Association.

Hudson is married to Boyd Matson. They live with their son and daughter in Upper Montclair, New Jersey.

[Date]

The following illustrates a newspaper-style bio that does not include personal information at the end:

Contact: Laura Epstein
(202) 555–1234

LILLIAN M. BEARD, M.D.

Dr. Lillian M. Beard, a practicing pediatrician in Washington D.C., is an Associate Clinical Professor of Pediatrics at the George Washington University School of Medicine and Health Sciences and an Assistant Professor at the Howard University College of Medicine.

Dr. Beard has held numerous leadership positions with medical associations. She is currently Chair of the National Medical Association's Council on Scientific Assembly. She has also served as Chair of the NMA's Section on Pediatrics, 1985–87. She was the Maryland State Director of the American Medical Women's Association, 1983–85.

Dr. Beard's extensive media experience includes serving as a spokesperson for the American Academy of Pediatrics, initially in the "Speak up for Young People" program that addressed many issues of adolescent sexuality, 1982–83, and, since 1985, as a national spokesperson on all health issues relating to infants, children, adolescents, and young adults. Dr. Beard writes a monthly column in *Good Housekeeping* magazine; has contributed on-air medical reports for WJLA-TV and WRC-TV in Washington, D.C.; and has appeared on nationally syndicated television programs, such as "Everyday" with Joan Lunden, "The Healthy Kids TV Show," and ABC's "The Home Show." Dr. Beard is a consultant to the Good Housekeeping Infants and Children Center and Carnation Nutritional Products Division.

Dr. Beard received her B.S. degree at Howard University, Washington, D.C., where she also received her M.D. degree. She completed a residency in Pediatrics and a fellowship in Child Development at Children's Hospital National Medical Center in Washington, D.C.

Feature bios are written in a more relaxed manner and read more like a magazine story, with additional elements of human interest, usually delivered through quotations from the subjects themselves.

Here is an example of a feature bio that contains all the information on the subject's history, but adds another dimension by way of his own reflections, including an opening comment from him:

NBC'S "SONNY SPOON" FEATURES AMERICAN HERO IN RECURRING ROLE; DISABLED VETERAN BOB WIELAND PORTRAYS JOHNNY SKATES

"I was eager to be part of an interesting new show, but I initially turned down the role," says disabled veteran Bob Wieland, who plays the recurring role of Johnny Skates on NBC's "Sonny Spoon," premiering Friday, February 12 (10:00–11:00 P.M. NYT). "I wasn't willing to compromise everything I work toward and represent by playing a bum," explains the double amputee. "The character was originally written as a panhandling derelict. I spend my life proving that a disability doesn't have to hold you back."

Impressed with Wieland's audition, the producers altered the character. Now, Johnny Skates is a respectable, streetwise informant who helps private detective Sonny Spoon (played by Mario Van Peebles) out of many jams and does his share of sleuthing on his trademark skateboard.

Commenting on his acting debut in "Sonny Spoon," Wieland says,

"I never intended to steer my career in this direction, having noticed that television doesn't cast too many double amputees. I didn't think the medium was ready. But when the producers contacted me, I was happy to give it a shot. With some coaching from Mario and Joe [costar Joe Shea], I'm learning on the job, and it's working out quite well."

Wieland, forty-one, is no stranger to the glare of TV lights and looming cameras. Since returning from service in Vietnam in 1969, he has emerged as an American hero. Viewers may recognize him from his well-publicized four-year "Walk for Hunger" (1982–86), in which he traversed the entire country on his hands at roughly one mile an hour and raised $315,000 for charities. Or perhaps they'll recall his spectacular last-place finish in the 1986 New York Marathon, when he crossed the finish line four days after the start of the race. Wieland doesn't let a disability ("Handicap is not in my vocabulary") get in the way of thinking big.

"This looks more serious than it is," says Wieland, referring to his disability. He's a four-time bantamweight world-champion power lifter who competes against able-bodied athletes. "Being disabled doesn't hinder me from doing everything I want to do."

In 1977, he broke the official world record in the bench press, lifting 303 pounds at a body weight of 122 pounds. He has received citations from the president and numerous mayors nationwide. In 1986 and 1987, respectively, *People* magazine and *Reader's Digest* named him one of America's living heroes.

Wieland is a longtime member of the President's Council on Physical Fitness and a motivational speaker who often visits high school students. His life changed drastically nineteen years ago when he stepped on a land mine while serving as an army combat medic. After recovering from the shock and trauma of losing both legs, Wieland decided he was going to set new world records in weight lifting. Ignoring the professional opinions that labeled him crazy, Wieland embarked on his inspirational journey.

Wieland, a native of Milwaukee, Wisconsin, has been married to dancer-actress Jackey Wieland for ten years and resides in Arcadia, California, with their three "children": a German shepherd, a poodle, and a terrier. He is working on his first book, *One Step at a Time*, due for publication in the fall of 1988.

CONTACT: Jane Doe, NBC (202) 555-1234
NBC-New York, 020888

Obituaries

As noted earlier, an obituary is the same as a biography, except that the lead of the obit offers details about the date and cause of the person's death.

Here is an example of how easily a bio can be converted into an obit:

ABC ELECTRIC'S VICE-PRESIDENT NICHOLAS ADDAMS DIES AT SIXTY-TWO

Dr. Nicholas H. Addams, Vice-President of Product Development for ABC Electric, died today in Fort Lee, New Jersey. He was sixty-two years old and died of heart failure, according to a family spokesperson.

A graduate of the Massachusetts Institute of Technology, Addams joined ABC Electric in 1982 as a special-projects director for the company's international division. He later served as the director of Consumer Products Development, beginning in June 1987. In that position, he coordinated the development of various electronic home conveniences—including breakthrough voice-activated home heating and lighting systems—as well as ABC Electric's tremendously successful home security systems, invisible fences, and audiovisual home entertainment centers.

In his most recent capacity as Vice-President, Addams was based in ABC's Passaic, New Jersey, headquarters and was responsible for approving and supervising the design and production of all products to be developed by ABC Electric for consumer and industrial use.

Addams came to ABC Electric from the New York industrial electronics company Omega Development, Inc., where he had been a design manager in the factory equipment division from January 1980 until January 1982. While serving in that role, he also became involved in the marketing end of the industry, by working as a technical planner, adviser, and lecturer at Omega's semiannual trade shows. From October 1978 until December 1980, he was the engineering manager in the robotics department, where he had started with the company as an engineer in February 1976.

A 1975 graduate of MIT with a doctorate in mechanical engineering, Addams earlier received an M.S. degree in computer science (1971) and a B.S. degree in physics (1969) from Rensselaer Polytechnic Institute in his native Troy, New York.

Addams is survived by his wife, Hillary.

CONTACT: John Doe, ABC Electric Publicity, (202) 555–1234
ABC Electric, [month, day, year]

Backgrounders

Backgrounders, as noted, are written on inanimate subjects, places, and products. Here is an example of a corporate backgrounder on the ABC Electric Company:

Background Information
ABC ELECTRIC INDUSTRIAL COMPANY, LTD.

ABC Electric Company, Ltd., of Tokyo, Japan, is one of the world's largest consumer electronics companies, with total sales in the past fiscal year of more than $54 billion.

ABC is known worldwide for its products marketed under the brand names of Highpro, Technoid, and Pulsar. The company is recognized as a leader in technological innovation and is the world's largest producer of home entertainment systems. In addition to audio and video equipment, ABC manufactures home appliances, communication and industrial equipment, electronics components, manufacturing systems, and related products. The company has a major presence in the office automation field as well.

Founded in 1907 by Hiro Yamada in Osaka, Japan, the company now has more than 10,000 employees worldwide and produces more than 9,000 products. In addition to its domestic operations, the organization has fifty-two manufacturing and forty-three sales companies operating overseas.

ABC places great emphasis on research and development, and last year spent close to $2 billion on R&D alone. Some of the more recent ABC innovations include a compact microvideo camera/recorder unit, an erasable optical memory disk recorder, industrial robotics, and other advanced technology products.

In the United States, the ABC Corporation of America is represented by its New York–based sales companies, Highpro, Technoid Industrial Company, and Pulsar, as well as its U.S.-based manufacturing companies, ABC Industrial Company in Athens, Georgia; Technoid Industries in Compton, California; and Pulsar Components Company in Knoxville, Tennessee.

This backgrounder succeeds for several reasons. It condenses lots of notable information into one page, and it offers the information simply, clearly, and painlessly. Let's examine each paragraph separately.

1. *Paragraph 1, the big picture.* The lead defines the subject of the bio right away (ABC) and makes an important statement ("one of the world's largest . . . ") that is immediately substantiated ("sales . . . of more than $54 billion").

2. *Paragraph 2, summary of scope.* The second paragraph describes the scope of the company's product line, again offering hard facts to back up claims.

3. *Paragraph 3, background.* The third paragraph summarizes the history of the company and tells a little about its structure, including the number of employees and sales operations.

4. *Paragraph 4, philosophy.* The fourth paragraph describes one of the company's priorities, research and development.

5. *Paragraph 5, conclusion.* The bio ends with the "boilerplate," a standard summary that explains some basics about the company, such as where its U.S. offices and factories are located.

It would have been easy to write about this company in eight or nine pages, but a reporter does not have time to wade through that much material. This backgrounder works because it offers only the most important information and does so in one page.

Notice that the language and sentence structure are varied; each sentence is a complete thought; and all sentences and paragraphs are logically connected to the ones preceding and following them. The writer also uses the present tense consistently throughout and does not assume that the reader already knows anything about the company.

In public relations, you are often in the storytelling business. All good stories have beginnings, middles, and ends, and all are interesting.

You should always know much more about your client than you'll be able to fit into the bio. Your job as a public relations writer is to learn everything you can about your client and then extract the most useful and important details, to create a brief, coherent story.

"I depend on biographies from public relations offices a lot," says

Andrew Edelstein, an editor for *New York Newsday*. "Sometimes I check the facts in them, while other reporters I know rely on them solely. Most reporters trust bios and use them more than press releases. I look for the kind of information I would ask about if given the opportunity to interview the client myself."

Writing the Bio

1. *Outline.* All good writing starts with a good outline. It doesn't have to be intricate, but it should be logical and complete. An outline is a map showing exactly where you are going and how you will get there. No writer, no matter how accomplished, should skip this all-important first stage.

2. *Command authority with the lead.* If you are going to get and keep your reader's attention, you must summarize the whole story with impact and authority in the first sentence and paragraph. The reader will know immediately from the lead whether the writer is in full control, has the facts, has a realistic perspective, and will make the reading experience worthwhile.

To write the lead, try pushing all your notes and written material aside. Step back from the details and ask yourself, "What does all this add up to? What is the larger meaning of this story? Is there one stunning fact that stands out beyond all the others—and does the fact relate to everything else in this story?"

You might also ask yourself, "How would I tell this to a friend, *conversationally?*" In other words, how would you generalize about the topic? That may help you say it more simply. A good lead will capture the essence of the biography without saying it in specific details.

3. *Clarify, simplify, condense.* Your job is to express ideas and information in the clearest and most logical way, with an economy of language. Take the complex and make it simple. The reader's reaction to confusion is always the same—boredom. Bore your readers and lose them. Be precise in choosing every word. Make sure the words you use mean exactly what you need to say—not almost, not overstated or understated. Also, make sure that each word and each sentence advances your story. It should not repeat information or just take up space. If a message can be communicated through a quotation, let the quotation say it, without using the information

again in the text. That will help the story tell itself. Use examples whenever possible. Use declarative sentences.

4. *Vary language and sentence structure.* One of the most common mistakes made by beginning writers is that they don't vary their language and sentence structure enough. This makes their copy monotonous. Notice if every sentence you write is in the order of noun, verb, noun, verb, noun, verb. That comes out sounding like "Dick runs fast. Jane runs faster." A more sophisticated example is "John Doe was appointed president of the St. Louis Chamber of Commerce in 1972. He had served as vice-president for five years previously. Doe is from Missouri." Boring, right? Here's a better way to condense that information and vary the language and sentence structure: "A native of Missouri, John Doe served as vice-president of the St. Louis Chamber of Commerce for five years, until his appointment as president, in 1972."

When you are writing at length about one subject, find a variety of words to identify it. For example, if you are writing a bio on a novelist, you may want to refer to that person occasionally as a *writer* or an *author*. You do not want to use *novelist* six times in the same paragraph, page, or story. It may help you to read your copy aloud and listen for repetitions and awkward phrases. Rewrite accordingly. Do not, however, force the use of synonyms at the expense of accuracy. For example, don't confuse *profits* with *funds* or substitute *revenues* for *earnings*. (A thesaurus can be a dangerous instrument; use it with discretion.)

5. *Connect thoughts.* Make sure that each sentence is connected to the one before and the one after, and that each paragraph flows logically from the one it succeeds. Transitions can come in many forms, such as comparisons, contrasts, analogies, or just the natural sequence of information. But information should never be introduced out of context.

6. *Attribute Quotations.* When you quote someone directly, attribute the quotation. Even if your biography covers only one person and your subject is the only person quoted throughout, you still must let the reader know who is speaking. Break quotes in natural places, not before the meaning or significance of the statement is clear. For example, " 'I will be forced,' says John Doe, 'to retire at age sixty-five'" is not a good way to interrupt the quotation for attribution. Better to write, " 'I will be forced to retire

at age sixty-five,' says John Doe." If you cite a quotation from a source—say, a newspaper article—always identify where and when it was published.

7. *Back up your claims.* When you make generalizations, substantiate them with facts. Attribute your claims to a source, or a standard of measurement. For example, you can't merely say that your company is the largest. Largest according to what—annual revenues? number of employees? amount of sales? Largest in the state, nation, or world? Be specific in qualifying statements. A performer may be the best soprano in America, *according* to *Opera News* magazine; a cable network may be the fastest growing over the past six months as *evidenced* by A. C. Nielsen ratings; or a company may be the largest manufacturer of microchips in the United States, with annual sales in excess of $1 billion.

8. *Use one tense.* Beginning writers often switch haphazardly between present and past tense. Choose one tense and try to remain in that tense throughout.

9. Assume nothing. Do not assume your reader knows what you are writing about or what you are trying to say. You can never be sure your writing is clear until another person has read your copy and has no questions about anything you've written. Identify all names, even if they are famous (for example, *actress* Meryl Streep, *comedian* Eddie Murphy). Also, define any technical terms you use. Clue readers in to all references.

By the time you write a biography or obit or backgrounder, you will know the subject intimately, but your reader will not. You must bring the story to the reader quickly, simply, and in a lively manner.

10. *Proofread carefully.* Careful proofreading of all public relations writing is essential. Double-check the spelling of all names and the accuracy of dates and facts. Do not rely solely on computer spell-check programs, because they do not flag a correctly spelled word that is wrong in the context of the sentence, such as the wrong verb tense or subject-verb agreement.

Fact Sheets

Fact sheets are a marvelous way to break down complicated information into easily grasped, bite-size pieces so that reporters and editors can easily find specific information that will be useful to them.

Here is a fact sheet about a cellular telephone called US WEST Cellular:

US WEST CELLULAR
FACT SHEET

DESCRIPTION	Cellular division of US WEST New-Vector Group, Inc., that markets its services under the name US WEST Cellular.
ADDRESS	3350 161st Avenue SE Bellevue, WA 98008 (206) 555–1234
BUSINESS	Cellular telephone service and equipment.
SIZE	US WEST NewVector Group has more than 1,800 employees.
OWNERSHIP	US WEST NewVector Group, a majority-owned subsidiary of US WEST, Inc.
KEY OFFICERS	John E. DeFeo, Chairman of the Board and CEO, US WEST NewVector Group Reynie U. Ortiz, President, US WEST NewVector Group Joseph L. Hughes, Vice-President, Marketing, US WEST NewVector Group
FOUNDED	Founded as NewVector Communications, Inc., in 1983; name officially changed in 1986 to US WEST NewVector Group, Inc.
PRODUCTS/SERVICES	Provides cellular service, mobile and portable cellular telephones, and other related cellular equipment under service name US WEST Cellular. Emphasizes quality service as competitive edge.
GEOGRAPHIC SIZE	US WEST Cellular service currently in twenty-seven MSA (Metropolitan Statistical Area) markets and twenty RSA (Rural Service Area) markets. US WEST NewVector Group is the tenth largest cellular company in the United States.

A fact sheet about the Commonwealth of Puerto Rico offers information in the following categories:

- Location
- Language
- Population
- Economy
- Government
- Entry formalities
- Climate
- History
- Accommodations
- Meetings and conventions
- Sightseeing
- Year-round festivals

Time Lines

When a chronology of developments or events is useful information, it is usually presented in a time line.

In NBC's press kit on the conclusion of Johnny Carson's thirty-year career as host of "The Tonight Show Starring Johnny Carson," the time line was written this way:

A TIME LINE OF SIGNIFICANT EVENTS

"The Tonight Show Starring Johnny Carson"

October 1, 1962	Show premieres from New York City, with Skitch Henderson leading the orchestra. Length of broadcast: one hour and forty-five minutes. Groucho Marx introduces Johnny Carson; guests are Mel Brooks, Joan Crawford, Rudy Vallee, and Tony Bennett.
1964	Debut of Carnac the Magnificent and Aunt Blabby; one of the longest sustained laughs in TV history when Ed Ames, demonstrating how to throw a tomahawk, hits a cardboard dummy in the crotch.
1966	Debut of the Mighty Carson Art Players; Milton Delugg becomes music conductor.
January 3, 1967	The show is reduced to ninety minutes in length.

1967	Doc Severinsen is promoted to music conductor; debut of Carson characters Carswell the Psychic and the Great Carsoni.
1968	Tommy Newsom named assistant music director; debut of Carson Character Faharishi, an Indian yogi.
December 17, 1969	Live, onstage wedding of Tiny Tim and Miss Vicki is seen by more than 45 million viewers.
1970	Fred de Cordova joins the show as producer.
1971	Debut of Carson character Art Fern and his "Tea Time Movie."
1972	"The Tonight Show Starring Johnny Carson" relocates from New York City to NBC in Burbank, California, and its permanent home, Studio One. The first annual anniversary show celebrates ten years of "The Tonight Show."
1973	Jack Benny actually *plays* his violin on the show.
1974	Writer-comedian Pat McCormack streaks across the "Tonight Show" stage.
1976	Fred Astaire sings "Life Is Beautiful."
1977	Debut of Carson character superpatriot Floyd R. Turbo; Alex Haley presents Carson with the comedian's genealogical records.
1980	The show is reduced to sixty minutes in length.
September 1983	Joan Rivers is named as a permanent guest host, a position she holds until spring 1986.
1984	Fred de Cordova is named executive producer.
September 1986	Jay Leno is named one of several guest hosts.

1987	"The Tonight Show" orchestra receives a Grammy Award. Jay Leno is named exclusive guest host.
August 1990	Producer Peter Lassally is named executive producer.
May 1991	Carson announces that his final date as host of "The Tonight Show Starring Johnny Carson" will be Friday, May 22, 1992.
June 6, 1991	Jay Leno is named to succeed Carson as host of "The Tonight Show," beginning Monday, May 25, 1992.

The Carnation Company offered the following time line to illustrate its history of milk products:

A TRADITION OF WHOLESOME MILK PRODUCTS

From its founding in 1899, Carnation Company has produced high-quality, nutritious milk products for American families. Carnation® Good Start™ infant formula and Carnation® Follow- Up Formula are only the latest in a long line of wholesome Carnation milk products.

In 1985, Carnation became part of Nestle, the world's largest food company and one of the world's largest sponsors of basic research in nutrition.

Today, the Nestle Carnation Food Company has a diverse line of more than 200 food products and sales of $3 billion. But as the following time line illustrates, Carnation built its enduring reputation for excellence on milk nutrition.

1899   E. A. Stuart takes over the operation of an evaporated milk plant in Kent, Washington, and establishes the Pacific Coast Condensed Milk Company, the beginning of Carnation.

1906   The company adopts "Milk from Contented Cows" as its slogan.

1916   Pacific Coast Condensed Milk Company changes its name to Carnation Milk Products Company.

1922   Purchase of a malted milk company.

1926   Carnation enters the fresh milk and ice cream business.

1927   Production of malted milk begins.

1929   Company changes its name to Carnation Company.

1954   Introduction of Carnation® Instant Non-Fat Dry Milk.

1955   Carnation "Gay Nineties" ice cream parlor opens at Disneyland in California.

1961   Introduction of Coffee-mate® Non-Dairy Creamer.

1964   Introduction of Carnation® Instant Breakfast.

1971   Introduction of Carnation® Hot Cocoa Mix.

1985   Carnation joins Nestle SA.

1988   Carnation® infant formulas introduced.

It can sometimes be useful to include a bibliography with a bio or backgrounder, offering a list of articles that have been published by or about the subject. Such a reference list saves the reporter a lot of time by allowing quick retrieval of an article, if needed.

Here is an excerpt from a bibliography included in a media kit for the internationally renowned art scientist Todd Siler:

BIBLIOGRAPHY (Partial List)

Breaking the Mind Barrier: The Artscience of Neurocosmology by Todd Siler (New York: Simon and Schuster, 1991), 416pp. with 100 b/w line drawings, End Notes, Index, Bibliography; *Breaking the Mind Barrier* (New York: Touchstone Books, 1992), high quality paperback, 416pp. with 100 b/w line drawings, End Notes, Index, Bibliography. This book is being translated in Spanish and published by Editorial Paidos in Buenos Aires; "Todd Siler en Buenos Aires. De la union del arte y la ciencia salio algo que todavia no se sabe bien ques es. Cual es el lenguaje del cerebro?", Domingo 14 de abril de 1991, pp. 2, 5, por Leonardo Tarifeno, El Cronista Cultural, Buenos Aires, Argentina. *Art in America*, April 1991, pp. 170, 172;

"Todd Siler at Feldman and the Boston Center for the Arts, New York/Boston," by Ann Wilson Lloyd. Tema Celeste, April 1991 pp. 92, 94;

"Todd Siler, Ronald Feldman Fine Arts," by Jude Schwendenwien. *The Boston Herald,* Tuesday, December 25, 1991;

"Siler's art explores in the mind," by Daniel Grant. *The Jerusalem Report,* February 14, 1991 p. 42;

"Renaissance Mensch, 'Artscientist' Todd Siler explores mind and universe," by Felice Maranz. *New York Times Book Review*, February 3, 1991, p. 35, "Noted with Pleasure," (on Siler's book *Breaking the Mind Barrier*).

Chapter Recap

In summary, the steps for writing a biography or backgrounder are as follows:

1. Work from a sensibly constructed outline.
2. Command authority with the lead.
3. Clarify, simplify, and condense.
4. Vary language and sentence structure.
5. Connect thoughts.
6. Attribute quotations.
7. Back up all your claims.
8. Use one tense.
9. Assume nothing on the part of the reader.
10. Proofread carefully.

Fact sheets organize complex information by category; time lines organize developments and events chronologically.

4

Speech Writing

From Your Pen to Their Lips

Public speaking is an effective way to gain recognition and to show leadership in one's company, community, or profession. In an age preoccupied with and fascinated by electronic technology, public speaking remains a powerful tool to inform or persuade a group of people. Public speeches often help set policy and act as a catalyst for action.

Good speeches are provocative and memorable, and they should be moving and easily understood. The best speeches gain a life well beyond their moment of delivery by influencing the audience, whether their purpose is to inspire, to motivate, or to encourage thought.

Regardless of the specific purpose of a speech—and each one should be custom-made to fit the personality of the speaker, the occasion of the speech, and the composition of the audience—every speech has to give the audience confidence in the speaker. A speech allows the speaker to be accessible and make an emotional connection with the audience; it is a chance to be more than just a corporate officer or political figurehead.

Every day, hundreds of speeches are given at a wide variety of events—from groundbreaking ceremonies and Wall Street analyst meetings to award dinners and congressional sessions, to name just a few. Public speaking is certainly not confined to politicians. Executives are also frequently called on to make speeches, which offer prime opportunities for positioning the executive and his or her company as a leader in their industry and/or community. It is usually the public relations writer who drafts the text of a speech.

John Cowan, editor of *Speechwriter's Newsletter,* based in Chicago, estimates that there are more than 3,500 people in corporate speech-writing positions in the United States and that their specialty can command salaries well into six figures. Very often, however, public relations generalists are also asked to write speeches. Whether it is one's exclusive specialty or only an occasional assignment, speech writing usually involves the writer with top management, major policy, and behind-the-scenes decisions, and it can require traveling to investigate or report on a subject.

Most executives are not professionally trained public speakers, and the very mention of a speech makes them nervous. Many speech writers also have their share of anxiety when it comes to preparing the speech. It is important to remember that the better the preparation, the less hazardous the whole process will be for the writer and the speaker alike.

Ad-libbing doesn't work. Each year during the Academy Awards ceremony, we see that even seasoned actors can go to pieces and stumble through acceptance speeches that are not scripted beforehand. The old show-business saying "If it ain't on the page, it ain't on the stage" summarizes the need for ample research, preparation, and rehearsal as safeguards to successful speeches. Writing for a *listener* is entirely different from writing for a *reader,* but a good writer can do both.

Speech writing is, indeed, a radical departure from other forms of writing. Many of the greatest literary treasures would make terrible speeches if read aloud. They may *read* well, but they don't *hear* well. In speech writing, the rules of written English must be replaced with those of conversational English.

"The two forms of writing are as different as an English sentence is from a German sentence," says Douglas Scott, a veteran speech writer who supplies major U.S. business leaders, such as Chrysler Chairman Lee Iacocca, with speeches. "The sentence that *looks* beautiful on the page can very often be weak, confusing, ambiguous, and totally ineffective when you *hear* it."

"New speech writers should use a lot of ellipsis points, a lot of double dashes," says William K. Lane, manager of Management Communications at General Electric, who writes and supervises about fifty speeches a year. "I was horrified by them at first. But suspension points free you from the bonds of grammar, of sentence structure; you can have run-on sentences, which help you convert to spoken English. In a speech, you can have a sentence that goes on for a long paragraph, but if it's broken up by pauses, it works. If you're going to print that in a magazine, you'll have to do a couple hours of work to put it back into written English."

Just as every story pitch you make is customized to fit the style, format, and focus of the media outlet you're soliciting, so too as mentioned earlier, is each speech uniquely tailored to suit the speaker, the occasion, and the audience. That means there is no precise formula for writing speeches. But there are certain steps each speech writer can take to ensure a coherent, appropriate script.

The keys to a successful speech are the following:

- Begin the project by interviewing the speaker.
- Learn about the place of delivery and the composition of the audience.
- Focus on a single theme.
- Obtain approval on the theme and the outline before writing the speech.
- Write for the human voice.
- Think of pleasing the audience, not just the speaker.
- Keep in mind any crucial controversy surrounding the speaker.
- Remember the importance of rehearsal.
- Hear the speech delivered.
- Research ways to recycle the speech so that it reaches a wider audience than those in attendance.

In the following section, we'll look at these ten general steps to approaching, preparing, and following through with a speech. Then, in the second part of this chapter, we'll examine the more specific, technical guidelines for writing the spoken word.

Speech Writing I: Ten Steps

Step 1: Interview the Speaker

Before you do anything else, talk to the person for whom you're writing the speech. Put yourself in a reporter's role. Take notes and tape-record the session. The more you learn at the first meeting, the less rethinking and rewriting you'll have to do later; however, even the most experienced writers rewrite a speech, and three to six drafts are not unusual.

Notice *how* the speaker speaks: What is the person's style and manner? Is he or she very precise, measured, and soft-spoken? aggressive and harsh? choppy or long-winded? What are the speaker's rhythms, and where is the emphasis? What kind of language choices are made—erudite or slang? Your script must follow the speaker's natural pattern of voice and expression. If you tape-record your conversation, you can replay the tape later, carefully analyze the answers to these questions, and take notes on other details during the interview.

Following are some important areas to cover in the interview with your speaker.

- *Discuss the audience.* Who will attend the speech? Will it be a trade group or the general public? How much background will you need to explain? Will there be company employees only, or will they bring their spouses? The nature of the occasion is important to know; it will dictate the tone of the speech. A U.S. Senate hearing is not a Friars Club roast. A meeting of the Securities and Exchange Commission is quite different from a meeting of the Screen Actors Guild. Think about your audience members—what are their ages, backgrounds, reference points, interests, dispositions, and attitudes?
- *Discuss topics.* Ask the speaker if he or she has any opinions on the possible topics to be covered in the speech. Have the speaker define the important issues facing your industry at the moment. Perhaps a particular news item or article stands out, suggesting an area of concern. Find out personal convictions— what really bothers the speaker? Don't panic if you both draw blanks. You may have to do more thinking about a topic and do some additional homework before you're even ready to suggest an idea.
- *Discuss attitude.* How does your speaker feel about giving the speech? Is it a treat or a chore? What happened the last time he or she gave a speech—how did it go over, and how did he or she feel?
- *Discuss length.* Determine how long the speech should be. Rarely can any speaker hold the attention of an audience for more

than twenty or twenty-five minutes. In speech writing, less is more. The Gettysburg address is a good historical example: Abraham Lincoln delivered it in three minutes. Edward Everett, his predecessor on the platform, spoke for two and a half hours. Which speech is remembered? Always know the time limit before you start researching and writing the speech. When you begin to write, keep this guide in mind: On average, six double-spaced pages with ample margins will take about ten minutes to say; three pages, about five minutes; and so forth.

Step 2: Interview the Sponsor

Talk with the people sponsoring the event at which your speaker will appear. Learn every detail involved: What time of the day or night will the speech be given? Will there be other speeches, and if so, by whom and on what topics? Will any other activity be competing with the speech? What will the audience be doing during the speech—standing or sitting? eating dinner? having drinks? studying printed material? listening to a translation? What will the audience have been doing before the speech, and what will the audience be doing after it? What is the context of the occasion—is it a regular event or one-time affair? If the former, you might ask the sponsor for samples of speeches given at prior occasions.

Whenever possible, visit or view the site where the speech will be given. Rhetoric that might work well in a large auditorium or amphitheater will be disastrous in an intimate, twenty-person conference room. As a speech writer, you'll need to write differently for audiences that are captive, as opposed to audiences that are free to come and go.

Step 3: Choose the Topic

When you emerge from the first meeting with your speaker without a decision on what the topic of the speech will be (which happens frequently), it is up to you to suggest a few possible subjects. And it is at this point that the speech writer goes from being an interpreter and translator to being a creator of ideas.

WHERE DO YOU GET IDEAS FOR A SPEECH? "Most executives don't have any ideas. They get an invitation to speak and ask, 'Should I do it? Is it good for the company?' The speech writer has to be broader than just a speech writer," says John E. Budd, Jr., president of the Omega Group, and former vice-president for external relations at the Emhart Corporation in Farmington, Connecticut. Budd, who once wrote an average of forty speeches a year notes that, "the speech writer should be very involved with the company or client. You have to have a feeling for trends and developments that affect the audience and then plot through your mind and ask, 'What will be *interesting?*'"

Budd advises that you're probably safe in never writing about how great the company or client is. Better, he says, to show some leadership. Although it's difficult to describe what's interesting or provocative until you get into specific instances, he offers this example:

> Emhart is a company whose product mix is pretty dull. It produces prosaic things like machinery that makes glass bottles and machinery that makes shoes, and so forth. Their executives make a fair amount of speeches, but they don't talk about Emhart. They address contemporary issues facing the industry or business in general.
>
> For instance, Emhart's chairman spoke in the Far East, and he talked about the role of the Pacific region as the center of gravity of economic progress in the future. He did not talk about Emhart's participation there. He spoke as a leader in business looking at the world.

In getting ideas for speeches, it helps to know a little bit about a lot of things. Do a lot of reading and try to keep up with everything that's happening.

Not all speeches invite unlimited possibilities for topics. There will be occasions that dictate what is appropriate to talk about. For example, if the occasion is the opening of a new factory, it would be logical to comment on what the new facility means to the company, to the community, and so forth. Or if an executive is unveiling a new product, it would behoove her or him to talk about it.

HOW MANY IDEAS CAN FIT COMFORTABLY IN A SPEECH? "Usually no more than one big idea can be the basis of a speech," maintains speech writer Carl Folta, senior director of corporate communications for Paramount Communications, Inc. "Too many ideas will confuse, complicate, or obscure the others." Veteran speech writer Douglas Scott agrees: "Enfolded in that one idea can be subideas advancing the main point. But as soon as you get into a laundry list of several large, important ideas, you're really in trouble. I'd advise anyone to trim them down as much as possible. You should be able to explain the thrust of the speech in one sentence, though it could be a fairly complex sentence."

According to General Electric's William Lane, you can measure the success of a speech by what the audience recalls. "If the audience walks out with one or two ideas that they remember, that you got across to them, then it's a tremendous success. One person may go home and say, 'General Electric is really into robots.' Then the speech worked."

"It is the *repetition* of ideas that makes the speech successful," says John Budd, Jr. "You can't have more than one or two big ideas. And you have to keep it simple."

Once you have learned all the background you need to know from the speaker and the sponsor and have decided on a topic or several topics to choose among, present them to the speaker for approval before proceeding any further.

Step 4: Research and Outline

After the topic of the speech has been approved, you are ready to research the subject and outline the structure and format of the speech. Good writing is based on thorough research and a careful outline, and speech writing is no exception.

RESEARCH. Check all references and resources available to you on the subject of your speech and any subjects closely related to it. Use a library or data bank to look up articles and books that relate to your speech. Check your office files for material that might be useful, review past speeches your client may have given on any associated subjects, and talk with people in your department and industry to get their thoughts and reactions to the topic.

On subjects that are timely or controversial, information can change quickly, so you must make sure you are entirely up to date. Don't make your speaker look foolish by not being current; make sure your facts are irrefutable. Your research is not finished until you completely understand the topic and have more information and background than you'll be able to use.

OUTLINE.   There are numerous ways to structure a speech, regardless of its content and length. The elementary three-part format of essays— introduce what you're going to say, say it, and then summarize what you've said—is a good general format for speeches. But the choices within that structure are almost limitless.

Here is a sample of a basic outline for a speech a company president might give to sales representatives at an annual sales meeting:

1. Welcoming remarks
   - Cordial greetings
   - Purpose of meeting
2. Report card on company growth
   - Sales figures this year
   - Sales figures compared with those of last year
   - Goals for coming year
3. Role of sales reps in relation to employees in other departments
   - Comparative remarks
   - Achievements
   - Goals for the future
4. Conclusion
   - Challenges ahead
   - How to meet them

An outline for a speech doesn't have to be intricate, but the more detailed and well organized it is, the more helpful it will be, by pointing to where and how specific ideas and information will be used.

Unlike readers, listeners cannot go back if they missed or didn't understand something. Help the listener by summing up complicated points, and make sure the meaning is crystal-clear.

The listener always needs help in knowing where the speech begins, where it's going, and when it ends—and so does the writer in putting it together.

Step 5: Make It Conversational, Keep It Simple, and Keep It Light

Speeches should be based on *conversational* language. The less formal, bloated, and academic the writing, the better the speech will be.

There are phrases and idioms that look like slang in print, but are wonderful when said aloud. Colloquialisms—expressions that are characteristic of familiar, informal conversation—should be used in speeches. On the other hand, beware of too much jargon.

Ralph Proodian, a New York–based speech consultant and coach, contributed an article to the *Wall Street Journal* titled "How to Make Your Next Speech One to Remember." Consider his examples of the difference between words to be read and words to be heard: " 'Since you are aware of the difficulties involved in the project . . . ' versus 'Since you know how hard this job will be . . . '; or 'I am fully aware of your critical role in this acquisition . . . ' versus 'I know this takeover wouldn't have worked without you. . . . ' "[1]

When writing the speech, ask yourself how the speaker would casually *say* this to a person next to him or her on a train. That should help you express the information more *conversationally* in the speech.

Keep the material simple and light, but not trite. Using humor and anecdotes helps keep a speech light—but beware of jokes. Most public speakers do not have the timing and delivery of stand-up comedians, and most are not natural storytellers either. But if humor can flow naturally out of the subject and is appropriate to all considerations, then it can be helpful.

Never resort to joke books. Humor must be "organic" to work: The classic, awful opening of a speech is when the speaker tells an irrelevant little joke and then says, "But seriously, folks . . . " Some executives resist using humor and anecdotes. They'll say, "I don't do humor; this is a *serious* speech." But you don't have to be pompous to be dignified. Being serious doesn't mean being dull. Injecting personal feelings, maybe even self-deprecating humor, is a way to attract and hold the attention of the audience.

THE LEAD. There are many ways to grab the attention of the listener at the start of a speech. You don't have to open with an arresting

[1] Ralph Proodian, "How to Make Your Next Speech One to Remember," *Wall Street Journal*, October 8, 1984.

question, a compelling anecdote, or an inflammatory statement that shocks or startles—but it's not necessarily bad if you do. More often, good speeches start with a salutation, a gracious acknowledgment by the speaker of where he or she is, who is being addressed, and why.

Often a speaker will begin with an amusing, self-deprecating comment to put the audience at ease by showing that the speaker doesn't take himself or herself too seriously. For example, when Lee Iacocca addressed the annual convention of the Century 21 Real Estate Corporation, he began this way:

> Thank you, [name of person who introduced him]. And good morning, ladies and gentlemen. It's an honor for me that you—the world's largest real-estate marketing organization—picked as your keynote speaker a car peddler—and what's more: a representative of Old Smokestack America.

Humor or lightheartedness can be a good way to warm up an audience and get attention quickly. This technique worked for Donald Keith, a high-level officer for the Pentagon, in his address to the Fort Worth Chapter Association of the army:

> Good evening. It's nice to be here in Fort Worth and away from the Pentagon—which the irreverent guys in the field sometimes call Fort Worthless.

A more straightforward approach can be used as well, diving right into the subject, as illustrated by John Budd in his speech to the Fairfield County Public Relations Association in Stamford, Connecticut, titled "Behind the Buzz Words: An Insider's Look at PR." He began like this:

> Currently, the public relations profession is deeply immersed in an all-out campaign to introduce public relations into the graduate school or MBA curriculum. The objective is noteworthy: to improve management's acceptance and understanding of what professionals in this area can contribute to the corporate goals and how to use such talents effectively. Academia does not tolerate new ideas easily, and public relations has long been pigeonholed in the journalism schools.

It is seldom advisable to use famous quotations in speeches. There are times, however, when they can be used successfully. Geraldine Ferraro's vice-presidential acceptance speech at the National Democratic Convention in 1984 made good use of a quotation in the lead:

> Ladies and gentlemen of the convention—my name is Geraldine Ferraro. I stand before you to proclaim tonight: America is a land where dreams can come true for all of us. As I stand here before the American people and think of the honor this great convention has bestowed upon me, I recall the words of Dr. Martin Luther King, Jr., who made America stronger by making America more free. He said: "Occasionally in life there are moments which cannot be explained by words. Their meaning can only be articulated by the inaudible language of the heart." Tonight is such a moment for me. My heart is filled with pride.

THE CONCLUSION. The end of a speech must be self-evident. The audience needs cues that it's almost over, and your speaker expects applause. There are numerous ways to signal the end of a speech. The speaker can say, "Before I leave you this evening, I'd like to review the main point . . . ," or "To conclude, I'd like to summarize . . . ", or "I know you're eager to hear the other guest speakers—and so am I— but before I go, I'd like to say . . . "

The best speeches have a unifying theme throughout, and the end of a speech should have a natural tie to the beginning. The main points should be summarized at the end of the speech.

Whenever possible, leave an audience with an optimistic feeling. Point to what can be achieved, what challenges lie ahead, and what rewards will ensue.

What does the whole speech mean to the speech giver? What does the speech mean to the audience? Those answers, stated simply, are usually points you should write into the conclusion.

Step 6: Personalize the Content

It's very important to please the speaker for whom you're writing, but that's not the only opinion that counts. The speech writer has to consider the audience. Will anybody really want to hear the speech?

Will anybody truly care? If you have personalized the content of the speech to the audience, the answer will be yes.

Personalizing the speech, and injecting emotion into it, can be very challenging, especially when you're dealing with lots of plain facts. But analyzing how the information affects the people listening to it should help you personalize it. If you have a diversified audience to reach, break down how the subject affects each group listening.

Step 7: Confront Controversy

Whether to address controversial subjects related to a speaker will always have to be decided on a case-by-case basis. But if your speaker has been invited because of that issue, you can't possibly avoid it. Confronting controversy can be a good way to clarify misinformation, offer background perhaps not covered in the press, or disarm a hostile audience. You do not want the audience thinking about one subject while your speaker addresses another, and you never want your speaker's credibility compromised. If a contentious subject is apt to come up in a question-and-answer period later, it's better to bring up the subject first and tackle it head-on.

Step 8: Test the Speech and Encourage Rehearsal

As soon as the first draft of the speech is written, read it aloud. Notice where your tongue gets twisted or you run out of breath, and rewrite accordingly. Then read it to someone else and ask to be stopped wherever the meaning isn't clear or confusion arises.

Before you show the speaker your first draft, test the speech by writing a news story based on it. If you have trouble writing even a paragraph or two, it may suggest that the speech is not very interesting and needs more work.

When the speaker is ready to review the speech, try to be there to listen. Find out what is not communicated clearly enough or where the speaker may feel uncomfortable. Also, make it your business to check any audiovisual, video, or other materials that will accompany the speech. Participate in technical rehearsals whenever possible.

Help your speaker by anticipating questions and comments the speech is likely to raise. Some speeches are followed by a question-and-answer period involving members of the press or the general audience, and the speaker should not be surprised or caught off guard by any of the questions. Supply related information if it is likely to be requested. When a speaker does not have specific information available on the spot, it is perfectly OK to have him or her say, "I don't have that information at the moment, but I will be happy to check on it and get back to you."

Step 9: Attend the Speech

Whenever possible, the speech writer should be present when the speech is given. Short of that, the writer should review a video- or audiotape of the speech. There is a great deal to be learned by hearing the speech delivered; it can always be better the next time around.

It is also helpful to hear people's reactions directly following the speech. Speech writers often comment that the most valuable reviews are heard in the restrooms afterward!

Step 10: Recycle the Speech

"When a speech is given, it fills the first requirements of news, in that someone did something somewhere," says John Budd. "And assuming there is something newsworthy said in the speech, there are countless ways to recycle it."

If the press is attending the speech, it is usually a good idea to have a copy of the speech available (sometimes it is distributed before the speech is given), along with a press release summarizing the most important points.

In addition to finding their way into newspaper stories, speeches can be reprinted in in-house publications, excerpted in trade and consumer magazine articles, taped for radio and television uses, and submitted to newsletters on current speeches.[2]

---

[2]Newsletters on speeches include *Vital Speeches,* published twice a month by City News Publishing Company, Southold, N.Y., and *Speechwriter's Newsletter,* published weekly by Lawrence Ragan Communications, Inc., Chicago, Ill.

Speech Writing II: Technical Guidelines

The following suggestions on format, grammar, and construction in speech writing will help the speaker read the speech more effectively, and the listener hear the speech more clearly.

- Never trust your speaker with an outline; write everything out, including all cues. If he or she is to hold up a plaque or point to a screen, for example, write those directions into the script, using parentheses.
- Write out dollar amounts ("12 million dollars," not "$12 million" or "$12,000,000"). Don't make your speaker count zeros.
- Submit copy that is clean and double-spaced and has reasonable margins. Your speaker may want to make notes. Some typewriters have changeable typeface elements that allow a larger typeface to be used. If you work with a word processor, you may wish to use a large font. Some speakers like to have their scripts typed in all capital letters. There is, however, a danger that punctuation can get lost.
- Underline emphasized words.
- Repeat nouns instead of using pronouns. ("The school is in trouble"; "The school needs your support"). Doing so helps to remind the listener of the subject and brings attention back to it, should the listener's mind wander.
- Write in parallel phrases and sentences ("Being here today gives me a chance to thank you, a chance to greet you, and a chance to bring you up to date"; "This is a government of the people, by the people, for the people").
- Use simple words and simple declarative sentences. Short, crisp sentences are the most dramatic form of writing; forget big words and flowery language. Avoid tongue-twisters. Substitute *especially* for *particularly, stubbornness* for *obstinacy*, and so forth.
- Beware of homophones, words that are pronounced alike but are different in meaning, such as *pier* and *peer, sew* and *sow*.
- Keep the subject and verb together. (Good: "Having learned of the new schedule, John arrived at class on time." Poor: "John, having learned of the new schedule, arrived at class on time.")

- Don't overload sentences with subordinate phrases and clauses. Clear, simple copy can transform lackluster speakers into attention-getters.
- Be specific, use examples, don't exaggerate, and don't overdramatize. Avoid overstated rhetoric and stick to basic, clear expression.
- Beware of quotes. A common first impulse is to refer to *Bartlett's Familiar Quotations* for a famous remark on the subject of your speech, but such quotes usually do not work. When a well-known quote is appropriate and worth using, set it up correctly, like this: "As President Kennedy said in his inaugural address, and I quote, 'Ask not what your country can do for you; ask what you can do for your country.' End quote."
- Avoid plagiarism. Not fully attributing a quote to its original source is plagiarism. Plagiarism is one of the worst sins of any kind of writing and can lead to public embarrassment. One of the most visible cases in recent years occurred when Senator Joseph Biden lost credibility as a candidate in the 1992 presidential primary over accusations of plagiarism.

Chapter Recap

Here again are the ten basic steps to writing a speech that is interesting and timely, and makes a useful comment on something of importance to the audience:

1. Interview the speaker.
2. Interview the sponsor.
3. Choose the topic.
4. Research and outline.
5. Make it conversational, keep it simple, and keep it light.
6. Personalize the content.
7. Confront controversy.
8. Test the speech and encourage rehearsal.
9. Attend the speech.
10. Recycle the speech.

5

Writing for Broadcast

Communicating in Pictures and Sound

The principles covered thus far in *The Public Relations Writer's Handbook* also apply to broadcast writing: Your ideas must be timely and newsworthy; your information must be accurate; your story must interest the intended audience; and your message must be stated clearly and concisely. In addition, broadcast writing imposes other considerations. This chapter will discuss the special concerns involved in writing broadcast news releases and pitch letters and in creating electronic media kits; it will also make recommendations for further reading.

A 1991 Roper poll found that 69 percent of all Americans get most of their news from television and that 15 percent rely on radio for news and information.[1] With more than 1,000 television stations and 8,000 radio stations nationwide,[2] the opportunities to advance your client's objectives through broadcast story placements and techniques are plentiful.

The most fundamental difference between writing for print media and writing for broadcast media is that in print, you are ultimately reaching *readers,* whereas in broadcasting, you are reaching *viewers* and *listeners.* To succeed in writing for the broadcast media, you must change your mind-set to think first of pictures and sound, rather than the printed word.

Television is based on moving pictures; radio is based on sound. In television, what is shown on the screen is generally more impor-

[1] The Roper Organization, "Sources of Most News," *Public Attitudes toward Television and Other Media in a Time of Change,* May 1991.
[2] Dodds Frank and Lisa Gubernick, "Beyond Ballyhoo," *Forbes,* September 23, 1985.

tant than what is said. The TV picture literally tells the story; the words simply reinforce it. The WABC-TV newsroom in New York City has a sign on the newsroom wall reminding reporters that If You Say It, Let's See It.

Radio news and features are based on "actualities," a term applied to the literal sound of anything other than the radio announcer's voice. An actuality, or ambient sound, can be another person speaking, the sound of traffic, a band in a parade, or the siren of a fire engine en route to a fire. Radio reporters often use actualities as background for their voice reports.

What this means to the public relations writer is that the opportunity to record video or sound, or the availability of existing video- or audiotape, should be mentioned in every story proposal or other correspondence to broadcasters. For example, if you issue a new release announcing the results of a new survey, a broadcast reporter will be reluctant to cover that story based on just a news release and a copy of the survey results. If, however, you can offer an interview with an expert spokesperson who is knowledgeable about the study, your chances for broadcast coverage are much greater.

Broadcast writing is ultimately a skill requiring great condensation. A broadcast writer must learn to summarize vast quantities of information in a short, conversational form of writing. To illustrate the difference between magazine writing and broadcast writing, here is a lead paragraph from a five-page *National Geographic* magazine story about an anthropological discovery in 1982:

> These were sights not to be forgotten: An ancient Roman lady emerging from a tomb of volcanic rock, her hand glorified still, after 1,903 years, by the shine of gold rings set with gemstones. A few feet away, an armed skeleton sprawling face down on the pumice-covered sand of a onetime beach. One end of a boat's hull breaking the surface and, beside it, perhaps the dead helmsman. In nearby chambers, a dozen, two dozen, maybe more, of the dead skeletons in anguished poses, a truly pathetic scene.[3]

[3]Joseph Judge, "A Buried Roman Town Gives Up Its Dead," *National Geographic*, December 1982.

That's a good magazine lead, highly descriptive and detailed. But when *Good Morning America* broadcast a segment on this story, featuring an interview with one of the anthropologists involved, the lead was written much differently:

> Nearly two thousand years ago, Mount Vesuvius erupted and destroyed the Italian city of Pompeii. It was long believed that the people living in the neighboring town had escaped. But a recent study sponsored by the National Geographic Society shows that more than five thousand people in the city of Herculaneum were also buried by volcanic ash and lava. Anthropologist Sara Bisel (BUY-CELL) has spent months digging up the remains of Herculaneum—and she's here with us today.[4]

Notice how quickly the broadcast lead summarizes the whole story, and how the script offers pronunciation tips for tricky names.

Here are the first two paragraphs of a news release issued to local *newspapers* by singer Lionel Richie when he made his debut as a solo artist at Radio City Music Hall in New York City:

FOR IMMEDIATE RELEASE:
LIONEL RICHIE ANNOUNCES SPECIAL CONCERT AT RADIO CITY
Proceeds Donated to Three New York Organizations
Midnight Show Added Thursday, October 13

In order to show his appreciation for five sold-out concerts at Radio City Music Hall October 11–14, Lionel Richie has added a special sixth performance at midnight on Thursday, October 13, at Radio City.

Richie is donating his proceeds from his sixth performance to three deserving New York organizations: the *Actor's Fund, Dance Theater of Harlem,* and *Symphony Space/Curriculum Arts Project.* He has also invited all performers currently appearing at the eighteen active Broadway theaters, as well as the Rockettes and members of the Dance Theater of Harlem, to be guests at the October 13 midnight concert.

"New York has shown me such love and appreciation," says Richie, "that I am happy to have a chance to give something back to

[4]Broadcast on "Good Morning America," November 11, 1982.

this great city, and I feel it's a joy to help in some small way." Richie also said, "There are so many deserving causes, but I picked these three recipients because they touched a common chord for me. *The Actor's Fund* helps take care of performers; the *Dance Theater of Harlem* is struggling against heavy odds to survive at this point—and continues to give black dancers a forum for their art; and the *Symphony Space Project* introduces children to all types of music.

Here is that same release condensed and converted into a broadcast pitch letter aimed at assignment editors in television newsrooms:

Dear Editor:

How does Lionel Richie say "thank you" to New York for selling out five concerts at Radio City Music Hall? By adding a special midnight show and donating the proceeds to three deserving New York organizations.

On Thursday, October 13, at 2:30 P.M., Richie will visit the *Dance Theater of Harlem,* located at 466 West 152d Street, where he will hand over a $10,000 check to Arthur Miller, the company's director. In addition, break dancers from Richie's concert show will perform in costume. Richie will be available for interviews and photo sessions after the presentation.

Richie will also be appearing at Junior High School #164 earlier that day to make a contribution to the *Symphony Space/Curriculum Arts Project.* Onstage at Radio City Thursday night, he will be awarding a check to the *Actor's Fund of New York.*

Attached is some additional information and Richie's complete itinerary for October 13. Feel free to contact me at [phone number].

Sincerely,

The broadcast version of Lionel Richie's story pitch makes the lead into a tease, offers a photo opportunity involving something visually exciting (dancers), has a local angle for New York news programs (local donations), and condenses the information into three short paragraphs.

Writing Broadcast News Releases and Pitch Letters

When writing news releases and pitch letters for broadcast segments—whether for local news programs or network talk shows—follow these guidelines:

- Write the lead as a tease.
- Offer the facts, but don't write the script.
- Suggest video/audiotaping opportunities.
- Keep it short and appropriate.
- Determine the category.

Write the Lead as a Tease

The lead sentence, as we've discussed in Chapters 1 and 2, grabs the reader's attention and compels him or her to continue reading. For broadcast purposes, the lead should be sharply honed to the broadcast style of what is called a tease.

"If you watch television, one of the techniques you'll notice is that of the tease," says Cliff Abromats, a veteran TV news director and producer who has worked in Miami, Cleveland, Philadelphia, and New York. "At eight o'clock, they'll promote the eleven o'clock news by telling you enough of the story to intrigue you, but they don't give it all away," he says. "Therefore, the first line of your press release or pitch letter has to be an enticing line that tells just enough about the story to force one to read on to get more details. If the first line is flat, if it doesn't make the assignment editor read on and say, 'Gee, I wonder what this is about, I wonder how we can make this interesting,' then it will land in the trash."

According to Abromats, the average TV newsroom in a major city receives about 250 news releases a day, of which two may get covered. "To even be considered," he says, "that first sentence has to be gangbusters."

Test your lead sentence by reading it aloud and following it with the phrase "Film at eleven," "The answer at eleven," or "Details tonight at eleven." For example, imagine you represent a consumer interest group and have discovered that your local salad bars use chemicals that have been known to cause health problems. Your broadcast news release lead might be this: "Your local salad bar could be making you sick [Details at eleven]." Or, say you represent a client who has been named Citizen of the Year by the Rotary Club of Columbus, Ohio. Your lead might be "Who's the best citizen in Columbus? [Answer at eleven]." And so forth.

Offer the Facts, but Don't Write the Script

The best broadcast writers tend to write in short, declarative sentences, using action verbs. And while it is a good idea to write this way and make your lead snappy in a broadcast tease style, it is *not* a good idea to present a public relations pitch in the form of a script. All reporters and newsrooms have their own style of writing and reporting, and you do more to irritate than interest them if you try to supply the story prewritten.

"I prefer to get the vital pieces of information in an intelligent letter that simply states the facts," says Dave Busiek, a reporter and anchor at KCCI-TV in Des Moines, Iowa. "But I resent it when I receive scripts from public relations writers with suggested wording. To me, it's insulting; it says, 'We have to spell this out for you airheads!' We do everything here," he says. "We either get stories from our CBS network, or we produce them ourselves."

You can also help a broadcast reporter by rounding off numbers ("nearly $10 million was raised," not "$9,693,292 was raised") and paraphrasing titles ("Jack Smith, head of the network," rather than "Jack Smith, executive vice-president and general manager of the network").

Suggest Video/Audiotaping Opportunities

In television, the visual appeal of a story is sometimes as important as its news or information value. After you've grabbed the attention of the editor in your letter or release, you must suggest ways to make your story visually exciting.

For example, if you're pitching a story about a television show or a theatrical production, invite the television crew to cover a rehearsal; if you're pitching a story on a manufacturing business, invite the television crew to visit the factory or plant to record the process by which the product is made.

TV cameras are particularly suited to recording processes, demonstrating how something is done, or showing an event as it happens. Action is what television reports look for. Similarly, radio reports need sounds to convey action.

In your broadcast story proposals, you should suggest opportunities to tape the subject. For example, if it's John Doe, Citizen of the Year, whom you are trying to get TV and radio reporters to cover, your pitch letter might be written this way:

Dear _____:

Who's the best citizen in Columbus? The Rotary Club has chosen John Doe, vice-president of ABC Electric, as its Citizen of the Year because of his contributions to community affairs.

Mr. Doe will be accepting the award next Monday, March 10, at a noontime luncheon in the Garden Room of the Regency Hotel. You are invited to attend the luncheon and tape his acceptance speech, in which he will talk about results of the fund-raising drive for the Columbus Community Hospital and plans for building a new children's wing. He will also be available for interviews both prior to and after the luncheon. And if your crew would like to follow him around for a "day-in-the-life" coverage, that could easily be arranged as well.

Enclosed is a press kit that includes Mr. Doe's biography and background on the award. I will call you next week to see if you can attend the luncheon. Meantime, don't hesitate to call me at [phone number] if I can assist in any way.

Sincerely,
[Name and title]

Keep it Short and Appropriate

Radio and television news coverage is often referred to as a "headline service" because of its brief treatment of subjects and events. Your broadcast proposals must also be extremely brief and to the point. In addition to condensing information, your material must be tailored to the show you are sending it to and to the length of the treatment it is likely to receive—anywhere from thirty seconds on radio to four or five minutes on television.

Hilary Kayle, a former senior researcher at NBC's "Today" show who often booked guests and assisted in assigning stories, emphasizes the importance of brevity and suitability:

I was offended by many of the form letters I received with program suggestions I could never use," she says. "It was obvious these people hadn't watched the show and had no concept of what I needed. A three-page, single-spaced letter with a press kit containing beautiful glossy photos didn't do me any good. It was the one-page letter that had a good idea, with something of interest to our viewers across the country, that would get my attention. I also needed to know if there was videotape available or what we could shoot ourselves.

In addition to well-known celebrities, Kayle says "Today" looks for guests who have credibility, authority, and a strong background in the field about which they will talk. The topic also has to be of interest to the public at large, have a consumer angle, and contain current news. Like other morning network programs, "Today" looks for stories based on events in the news, segments based on products that have fixed release dates—such as movies or books—or general human interest and consumer interest topics. A likely guest might be a psychologist discussing why people lie, or a business adviser talking about how to manage money.

Like many news and entertainment-show editors and talent bookers, Bob Dolce, former longtime talent coordinator for "The Tonight Show Starring Johnny Carson," preferred to get a phone query first, before any written material is sent. Being brief and concise is just as important on the phone as it is in writing. Says Dolce: "A lot of people take too long to present a client. I know within three minutes if you've got a guest for our show or not. We were interested in people who had interesting anecdotes that had a beginning, a middle, and an end. And we wanted a story that nobody else could have told. I call those stories 'fingerprints.' We basically looked for something that nobody had said before."

There are no universal criteria for what makes a story or guest eligible for broadcast coverage. Even two local news shows in the same market may have different formats and philosophies. One may have an entertainment, or soft news, focus, with an emphasis on in-studio interviews. The other may be more devoted to hard news, with an emphasis on field reports. For the former, actors Jane Fonda or Paul Newman would be ideal subjects; for the latter, only a mayor or governor might do.

For example, "The Arsenio Hall Show" and Ted Koppel's "Nightline" are both nationally broadcast shows that rely on in-studio interviews, but clearly, the types of guests interviewed on each are vastly different. Arsenio Hall has a distinct penchant for celebrity interviews, while Koppel wants individuals who can bring insight into timely issues. It's important that you recognize those differences before you write broadcast story proposals.

Determine the Category

Local news programs generally cover stories that fall into five basic categories:

1. Crises and natural disasters
2. Medical stories concerning health and well-being
3. Economic stories that affect more than just the financial community
4. Good Samaritan stories about people who have done something positive for their communities
5. Clever or humorous stories that entertain rather than just inform

Before you write a broadcast news release or pitch letter, check to see which of the above categories the subject fits into and what video- or audiotaping opportunity it offers. If your story doesn't qualify in some broad sense, perhaps you need to review the way you are presenting it.

Creating Scripts for Electronic Media Kits

There are some forms of broadcast public relations writing in which creating a script is required. These include video news releases, public service announcements, promotional films, and audiovisual presentations.

Video News Releases

A video news release (VNR)—also referred to as an electronic press release (EPR)—is a client-sponsored video that presents a controlled message using a news angle. Entertainment, sports, and medicine are the most popular subjects of VNRs.[5]

Generally, a VNR runs in length between ninety seconds and two minutes. It can be a single spot or a multipart series, depending on the story and its news value. For the most part, a VNR is used as a filler on a slow television news day or as a feature story. Many television reporters say they will use a VNR only if it covers a subject they're interested in and there's absolutely no way they can videotape it themselves.

There are three basic uses for a VNR:

1. To promote a product or service by tying it to a newsworthy event.
2. To disseminate information quickly in a crisis.
3. To publicize a corporate announcement.

The running time of electronic press kits can be longer than VNRs. Both VNRs and EPKs can be produced with and without voice-overs.

Public Service Announcements

The public service announcement (PSA) blurs even further the line between news and advertising. A PSA is a short spot (anywhere from ten to sixty seconds in length) that television and radio stations broadcast at no charge to the sponsor. Nonprofit organizations place the most PSAs on the air, but commercial organizations may also promote nonprofit activities, causes, or events via PSAs.

It is through PSAs that broadcast stations fulfill their obligation, as outlined by the Federal Communications Commission (FCC), to serve the community and public interest. PSAs usually publicize community events and health or safety tips. The people at radio and television stations who decide what gets aired in the form of a PSA usually have titles such as Public Affairs Director or Public Service Manager.

A PSA can be submitted on paper in script form, or it can be produced on audiotape for radio or on videotape for television. Sometimes the public relations representative will provide both script and tape.

[5]Alissa Rubin, "Video News Releases: Whose News Is It?" *Public Relations Journal,* October 1985, p. 19.

Here are two examples of PSAs that were carried by radio stations:

Fathers have babies too. CD-101.9 wants you to know the March of Dimes has prepared a brochure to help fathers through pregnancy. To get a free copy, call [telephone number].

Does your child seem to have ear infections often? or sinus infections? and doesn't seem to respond to medication? CD-101.9 wants you to know these could be signs of primary immune deficiency, a genetic disorder that cripples the immune system. To find out more about it, call [telephone number].

Here are two examples of PSAs that were broadcast on network television:

THE MORE YOU KNOW
SPOT #7/STAY IN SCHOOL
Talent: Stepfanie Kramer
TV: 30
RECORDED COPY

SUPER
DON'T BE A FOOL.
STAY IN SCHOOL.

TALENT
You think staying in school is tough? Tell you what's tougher: *not* staying in school. As a high school graduate, you can look forward to a career . . . even college. As a dropout, you can look forward to a life of low-paying jobs and rejection.

The more you know how hard things are for dropouts, the more you realize that paying dues for a few years is a lot smarter than paying dues for a lifetime.

END FILM, MUSIC, SUPER

THE MORE YOU KNOW
SPOT #5/DRINKING AND DRIVING
Talent: Rhea Perlman
TV: 30
RECORDED COPY

SUPER
ACTIONS SPEAK LOUDER THAN WORDS.

TALENT
Have you ever noticed that kids don't listen to what we say, they listen to what we do? Too many of them think it's OK to drink and drive because too many of us think it's OK. Don't you think it's time we parents grew up and stopped asking our children to do what we're not willing to do? The more you know about kids, the more you know that if we don't want them to start drinking and driving, we're going to have to stop.

END FILM, MUSIC, SUPER

The pages of broadcast scripts are usually divided into left and right sides, with the text on one half only. That helps the writer keep sentences short, and therefore more easily spoken, with plenty of opportunities for breathing. For television, the page division also allows one side to be used for noting what is on the screen (video) as the text is being read (audio). A one-page, double-spaced, typewritten script on the right side equals approximately thirty seconds of spoken copy.

Broadcast scripts have their own technical language, which is usually abbreviated. Here are some of the most common shorthand examples:

SOF = sound on film
SFX = special effects
VO = voice-over
CU = close-up
CHYRON = text on screen
OC = on camera
MS = medium shot
SIL = silent film
ECU = extreme close shot
B-roll = scenic pans, ambient sound, interview responses (all without the reporter)
Super = print on screen (such as someone's name and title)
Wipe = totally new picture

Here is an example of a script for a video news release disseminated nationally by the public relations agency Burson Marsteller. This VNR script was created to publicize National Breast-Cancer

Awareness Week and was sponsored by a grant from Stuart Pharmaceuticals.

NATIONAL BREAST-CANCER AWARENESS WEEK VNR
TIME: 1:50

VIDEO	AUDIO
	VO #1
BETTY FORD AT HOME WITH SUSAN AND THE KIDS	BETTY FORD FOUGHT BREAST CANCER A DECADE AGO, AND WON. NOW HER DAUGHTER SUSAN FORD VANCE IS CONTINUING THE FIGHT . . . BY LAUNCHING THE FIRST NATIONAL BREAST-CANCER AWARENESS WEEK, WHICH BEGINS OCTOBER 21 . . .
B-ROLL CONTINUES OF FORDS SUPER; SUSAN FORD VANCE	(sound bite) SUSAN FORD VANCE: "The reason that I'm involved in this program is that my mother did have breast cancer ten years ago, and of course it did have an effect on me. I practice breast self-examination on a regular basis, and I think all women need to learn how to do it so that they don't have to worry the way that we all have to."
WIPE GRAPHIC: 1 OUT OF 11 WOMEN	VO #2 THE WORD ON BREAST CANCER IS SIMPLE: . . . ONE OUT OF EVERY ELEVEN WOMEN WILL GET IT, AND
GRAPHIC: 90% DISCOVER IT THEMSELVES GRAPHIC: WOMEN DOING BREAST SELF-EXAM	90 PERCENT OF THOSE WOMEN WILL DISCOVER IT THEMSELVES, . . . MOSTLY BY ACCIDENT. ALTHOUGH EARLY DETECTION CAN SAVE LIVES, A MAJORITY OF WOMEN DO NOT TAKE THE PRECAUTIONARY STEPS. . . . (sound bite)

HEADCUT: DIANE BLUM
SUPER: DIANE BLUM, NATIONAL
CANCER FOUNDATION

DIANE BLUM: "The reason that women don't practice breast self-exam is that a lot of women tell you they don't have any confidence in doing it. They examine their breasts every month and they don't know what they're feeling." (sound up)

B-ROLL: YWCA WORKSHOP

JOYCE GREEN: "Now, when your hands are in place, you make a slight circular motion." (sound under)
VO #3

B-ROLL CONTINUES SHOTS OF
YWCA EARLY-DETECTION CLINIC

FREE, EARLY-DETECTION WORK-SHOPS LIKE THIS ONE ARE BEING OFFERED AT SELECTED YWCAs NA-TIONWIDE. THE WEEK IS SPON-SORED BY THE NATIONAL CAN-CER FOUNDATION AND STUART PHARMACEUTICALS. WOMEN ARE TAUGHT BY PROFESSIONALS HOW TO PERFORM BREAST SELF-EXAMS. MANY DOCTORS AGREE, AN IN-CREASE IN EARLY DETECTION WILL ALSO INCREASE BREAST-CANCER TREATMENT OPTIONS. . . . (sound bite)

HEADCUT: DR. HARVEY LERNER
SUPER: HARVEY J. LERNER, M.D.
GERMANTOWN HOSPITAL,
PHILADELPHIA

DR. LERNER: "The reward for finding an early or small breast cancer is that of having many treatment options avail-able, and if the woman wishes, she may have a breast-conservation operation and her breasts may look identical and symmetrical."
VO #4

GRAPHIC: WOMEN BEING
EXAMINED

DR. LERNER STRESSES THE COMBI-NATION OF BREAST SELF-EXAM,

FREEZE: B-ROLL CHYRON OVER FREEZE	REGULAR MEDICAL CHECKUPS, AND MAMMOGRAPHY FOR EFFECTIVE EARLY DETECTION. THESE STEPS . . .
	. . . OFFER WOMEN OF ALL GENERATIONS BETTER TREATMENT OPTIONS AND. . . .
B-ROLL: FORDS AT HOME	. . . A GREATER CHANCE OF SURVIVAL. I'M CATHERINE COWDERY REPORTING.

This VNR offered television news directors two options: to use the video with a prerecorded announcer's voice narrating the story or to use just the video so that each station could use its own announcer's voice-over.

Promotional Films

There are broadcast versions of many of the pubic relations writing forms discussed in this book. For example, a client may want a film produced to tell the company's history (the backgrounder), to inform customers about its services or the financial community about its growth and future prospects (the brochure or annual report), or to show community involvement (the PSA).

Many large public relations firms have in-house departments that work exclusively on film and videotape presentations. Smaller firms and clients hire independent production companies to do the production.

Promotional films are often termed *industrials, trailers, teasers, promos,* and *previews.* Scripts are sometimes written after the tape is shot; other times, they are drafted well in advance of production. Whichever way the script is created, it is almost always a highly collaborative effort that goes through many hands and many drafts.

Audiovisual Presentations

The main use of an audiovisual presentation is to support a speech. That is, a slide is projected onto a screen in coordination with what the speaker is saying. The term *audiovisual* is usually referred to in abbreviation as *AV*.

AV presentations generally run in length from one to seven minutes and can use up to one hundred slide projectors at once. Sometimes, the choice of slide images is suggested by a script; other times, an AV presentation may be all images and music, with no words spoken at all.

The main advantage of an AV presentation over a film is that slides can be changed easily up to the last minute, whereas film or video editing is more complicated and time-consuming.

Here is the beginning of a speech that uses slides, which are noted in parentheses. The title of the speech is "Renewing Interest: How Can Retention Marketing Work for You?" and it was presented by Kathy Canavan, vice-president of marketing, Group W Satellite Communications, at the National Cable Television Association meeting.

> I'd like to start by reading you a brief statement that appeared in *TV Guide* last fall. It was just before The Nashville Network was about to carry twelve live hours of the FarmAid concert featuring fifty-seven star performers. And the editors of *TV Guide* commented on that upcoming television event this way, and I quote: *(SLIDE 1)*
>
> "If you live in one of the 45 million or so U.S. households that don't happen to subscribe to cable television—and The Nashville Network in particular—consider yourself a second-class citizen." End quote.
>
> I think I'm safe in assuming that all of us here today agree with that statement, and embrace *TV Guide's* opinion. Without cable, the television viewer is a second-class citizen.
>
> Our job, however, is to make every cable subscriber and potential subscriber agree that cable is a must-have item in their household. The fact is that cable does offer a wide range of high-quality alternative programming. And much of that programming is *original*. Cable offers *exclusive program formats*. *(SLIDE 2)*

Every public relations agency and department has its own style of script writing and formatting for each type of broadcast writing. The main point to remember in writing broadcast scripts is that the words will be spoken and, therefore, must be written in a short, conversational style. And when writing video scripts, you must always consider what will be pictured on the screen and how the words will relate to the images.

Recommended Reading

Many trade and several consumer publications are devoted to reporting on the broadcast industry. The include *Variety, Broadcasting, Electronic Media, Multichannel News,* and *TV Guide.* Newsletters offering useful information include the *Paul Kagan Newsletter, Larimi PR Contacts, Media Newskeys,* and the *PR Aids Party Line.*

Chapter Recap

In review, the guidelines to writing broadcast news releases and pitch letters are as follows:

- Write the lead as a tease.
- Offer the facts, but don't write the script.
- Suggest video/audiotaping opportunities.
- Keep it short and appropriate.
- Determine the category.

6

Special Events

The Art of Getting Noticed

In order for any event, public or private, to become a major news story, a story that dominates the media for weeks or months, the event and the coverage of the event must acquire a key ingredient. Without that ingredient the story drifts and eventually withers. The ingredient is reaction— broad public reaction. Until there is reaction, either in the form of growing attention in the press, or visible public attention of other kinds, the event is like an airplane moving along an endless runway, unable to get up enough speed to take off. Some events are sufficiently momentous to compel substantial and varied reaction from the time they occur until far into the future. Just as often, though, reaction develops gradually, and then is sharply accelerated by some form of catalyst—a particular news article or a subsequent event.

—David McClintick, *Indecent Exposure*

As a public relations representative, you are often responsible for creating events that bring attention to your client or cause. In proposing and planning an event, the single most important question you must always ask yourself is, "Will anybody care?" Or, to use David McClintick's phrase, "How broad will the public reaction be"? Sometimes, you will need only your local community to care; other times, you will want the entire country to take notice. As you read news stories, listen to radio reports, or watch television news programs, try to determine how many "news items" come from a public relations event. Examples of such events range from dances, contests, parades, and fashion shows to political conventions, debates, protest marches, concerts, and ceremonies of every kind.

To many people, the special event is the best-understood aspect of public relations. The news conference, the press party, junket, and the publicity tour are the most widely used vehicles to inform the media, which, in turn, inform the public.

In this chapter, we will examine these special events and the writing skills required for creating invitation copy, media alerts, photo opportunity alerts, and media kits.

The News Conference

Perhaps the most common public relations event is the news conference. To hold a news conference essentially means to gather the media at a designated place and time so that they can hear a significant and newsworthy announcement and ask questions. The news conference is one of the most straightforward methods of generating publicity.

The most important part of a news conference is the announcement being made. Regardless of how much hoopla accompanies a news conference, if the announcement is not newsworthy, the coverage will be minimal at best.

News Conference Checklist

Begin with a checklist. Because news conferences, like all special events, are detail-intensive, it is useful to make a list of all items that might need attention.

Imagine you will be holding a news conference to announce a new television set that is the size of a credit card. Your checklist could look like this:

- Invitation list—press and others
- Time and date: possible conflicts
- Invitations
- Media alert
- Photo opportunity alert
- Callbacks to invited press members to firm up attendance
- Daybooks
- Media kit
    Speeches
    Main announcement release
    Technology release
    Executive bios

Company backgrounder/fact sheet
Photos/captions
- Possible questions from the media and draft of answers
- On-site arrangements
Room rental
Menu
Audiovisual equipment
Electrical hookups
Signage
Name badges
Sign-in books
- Rehearsal
- The PR Newswire and the Businesswire
- Follow-up

Now let's examine each item on the checklist.

Invitation List

Every event requires its own list of journalists who should be invited. In addition to the media, it is often appropriate to invite others, such as prominent industry figures, celebrities, or client-related management representatives. Special considerations for the media list include the following:

- *Location.* It doesn't make sense to invite a TV reporter in Omaha to a news conference in Dallas. Invite only those people who would not have to travel unreasonably far.
- *Subject Matter.* A food editor will not be interested in the "Credit-Card TV" announcement. Make sure you invite only those journalists who would have an interest in covering the subject of the news conference.
- *Visuals.* Will television crews be able to tape a good story at the news conference? Does the event offer good photo opportunities? If you invite television crews and photographers, make sure you offer more than "talking heads." (See Chapter 5 for information on broadcast publicity.)

Once you have considered these elements, it is helpful to divide your media list into categories. For the "Credit-Card TV" news conference, your media list could be divided into the following categories:

- General business publications
- Local newspapers
- Wire services
- Audiovideo publications
- Broadcasting trade publications
- Science/technology publications
- Consumer publications
- Local and network television news programs

(To review the construction of a media list, see Appendix B.)

Time and Date: Possible Conflicts

When selecting the time and date of an event, you must consider several factors that could affect attendance. You do not want to hold the conference on a major holiday or the day before or after a long weekend.

Next, as best you can, make sure the event does not conflict with other activities that will be drawing journalists that day. For the "Credit-Card TV" announcement, it would be disastrous to hold the news conference during the same week as the Winter or Summer Consumer Electronics Show, which attracts all of the major media covering consumer electronics.

In April 1985, a well-known manufacturer of office copiers held a news conference to announce the results of a survey on secretarial attitudes toward office automation. On the same day, Coca-Cola announced its "new Coke." Not surprisingly, attendance at the survey announcement was disappointingly low.

The time of the event is also important. Deadlines for morning-newspaper reporters and evening-television news reporters are in the afternoon, so if you want them to attend, you had better hold your event in the morning. But if your goal is to attract columnists, weekly and monthly magazine editors, or feature television reporters, you may want to hold a press party in the afternoon or evening. A press party is more relaxed than a news conference and, as the name implies, is more festive. It is usually held to celebrate or mark a special occasion, and food, drink, and entertainment are customarily provided.

Invitations

The invitation copy and presentation are a crucial part of generating attendance and media coverage for a special event. Some reporters receive up to fifty pieces of mail a day from public relations people. By necessity, they often sort through their mail quickly, making fast decisions on whether to throw something in the trash or set it aside for a closer look.

One of the best ways to make sure your invitation will be opened and read is to use *hand-addressed* envelopes to send printed invitations that incorporate your client's name or logo. Many journalists have remarked that they usually open personalized invitations.

An invitation is similar to a pitch letter and it should get right to the point. Essentially, it should answer the following questions:

- What is the purpose of the event?
- Where is it being held?
- When is it being held?
- Why should a reporter attend? (What can be learned on-site that cannot be conveyed on paper or by telephone?)
- Will any type of food or drink be served?
- Who should be contacted for more information?

Invitation copy condenses a lot of information in a small amount of space. For the "Credit-Card TV" announcement, your invitation might be written this way:

You are cordially invited to attend the unveiling of
the world's smallest color television
on
Tuesday, November 8,
from 10:00 A.M. to noon
Greentree Hotel, Palace Suite
123 Elm Avenue
Chicago, Illinois
RSVP: John Doe
(202) 555–1234

ABC Electric, America's largest producer of color TV sets, will demonstrate its latest breakthrough in television technology. William Jones, the president of ABC Electric, will be available to answer questions.

Lunch will be served after the conference.

You may also want to include a reply card, which would look like this:

Name: [Prewritten]

☐ Yes, I will attend the conference.
☐ No, I cannot attend the conference, but please send a press kit.
☐ No, I cannot attend the conference, and do not need a press kit.

The card, essentially a postcard, should have your address printed on the other side, and it should be *stamped*.

In some cases, the invitation copy should not divulge the news content of the news conference beforehand. This means you must be vague about the announcement but enticing nonetheless. In such a case, an invitation might read like this:

You are cordially invited to attend a news conference
hosted by ABC Electric.
The company will make a significant announcement
concerning TV technology
on
Tuesday, November 8,
from 10:00 A.M. to noon
Greentree Hotel, Palace Suite
123 Elm Avenue
Chicago, Illinois
RSVP: John Doe
(202) 555–1234

ABC Electric, America's largest producer of color TV sets, will demonstrate its latest breakthrough in television technology. William Jones, the president of ABC Electric, will be available to answer questions.
Lunch will be served after the conference.

The invitation copy will be written differently for parties, concerts, sporting events and other affairs, but if you include the vital information listed above, your invitation is likely to produce results. (See Chapter 8 for a discussion of how copy is prepared for printing.)

Media Alert

A media alert—also called a news advisory or a tip sheet—provides a brief summary of the basic facts of an event and is often used to follow up the printed invitation or replace it when there is no budget or time for one.

Media alerts should never be more than one page in length, and they should contain the same information as invitations.

Western Union mailgrams are an effective though costly method of distributing media alerts. The mailgrams are delivered overnight, and journalists almost always open them.

Media alerts should always answer the fundamental questions *who, what, where,* and *when.* More often than not, this information is printed in boldfaced type to stand out quickly to the reader.

For example, here's how a media alert for your "Credit-Card TV"conference might look:

MEDIA ALERT FROM ABC ELECTRIC

CONTACT: John Doe
(202) 555–1234

What: ABC Electric will unveil the world's smallest color TV set and demonstrate the latest in TV technology.

Where: Greentree Hotel, Palace Suite, 123 Elm Avenue, Chicago, Illinois

When: Tuesday, November 8, from 10:00 A.M. to noon

Who: Bill Jones, the president of ABC Electric, will be available to answer questions.

BACKGROUND INFORMATION

ABC Electric is America's largest producer of color TV sets. The company had annual sales last year of $2 billion, and has more than 3,500 employees throughout the world. In the past year it has introduced several signficant technological breakthroughs, including digital TV sets, stereo TV, and three-dimensional TV technology.

All invitations or alerts should grab attention right away. They should never be long-winded or flowery.

Photo Opportunity Alert

A photo opportunity alert, or photo tip sheet, is a media alert customized to attract television or photo coverage. When you are sending media alerts (or invitations) to television reporters or print photographers, your copy must stress the visual aspects of the event. Thus, your alert for the "Credit-Card TV" announcement would be written with an emphasis placed on the visuals—or photo opportunities—offered by the new product. For example:

> *Photo Opportunity:* ABC Electric will show a TV set that is so small it can be slipped into a wallet.

Good visuals can be tremendously effective. When the San Francisco area chapter of the Boy Scouts of America wanted to attract publicity to help its fund-raising drive, the chapter members decided to conduct a demonstration of camping skills, such as campfire building, cooking, knot tying, and tent pitching. To make the event attractive to the media, they added one special twist: The demonstration was held on top of the Embarcadero Center in downtown San Francisco.

Following is an excerpt from the media advisory written by Ron Walsh of the San Francisco Bay Area Council of the Boy Scouts of America:

> Mention Boy Scouts, and the average American thinks of forests, mountains, and a roaring campfire.
> But on April 1, a group of San Francisco scouts begins a three-day expedition not in the wilderness, but on the top of a forty-five-story skyscraper.
> The twenty scouts will spend seventy-five hours camped out on the roof of 4 Embarcadero Center, a high-rise building overlooking San Francisco Bay.

The publicity results for the Boy Scouts were enormous. According to Walsh, photos appeared in dozens of daily newspapers across the United States, and televised coverage ran on both network and local news programs.

For some events, you will want to write two different invitations or media alerts: one for print media and one for broadcast reporters and photographers.

Callbacks

Once your invitation or alert has been sent out, you should begin conducting callbacks approximately one week after your mailing. Callbacks are necessary because people often do not respond to the invitations, and because invitations and alerts can easily be overlooked or lost in the mail.

After completing your callbacks, make an alphabetical list of everyone who will be attending. This is crucial for planning the amount of food to be served and the number of press kits to prepare, as well as for typing out name badges for attendees. Keep an organized list of those *not* attending the event, and their reasons. That will help you plan subsequent events and avoid wasted effort. Send press kits to those interested in the story but unable to attend.

Daybooks

The two major wire services, the Associated Press and City News Service, issue daybooks, daily schedules of news events. Assignment editors and reporters keep a watchful eye on daybooks, and you should always try to have your news event included in them. To be considered for the daybook listings, send a brief paragraph describing your event to the daybook editor at each of the wire services, and enclose more detailed information on the subject as well.

The daybook copy should run on the wire services *the day before* your event so that it can be seen twice: in the afternoon daybook on the day before the event, and in the morning daybook on the day of the event.

Your daybook alert for the "Credit-Card TV" announcement might look like this:

NEWS CONFERENCE ON WORLD'S SMALLEST COLOR TV

ABC Electric will unveil the world's smallest color TV. The TV is the size of a credit card and can fit into a shirt pocket or wallet. The conference will take place in the Palace Suite at the Greentree Hotel, from 10:00 A.M. to noon. William Jones, the president of ABC Electric, will be available to answer questions. Contact John Doe at (212) 555-3535 for further information.

It helps to call the daybook editor to alert him or her to the event and to confirm that the alert was received.

Media Kit

Media kits must be available at any news-oriented special event. The kits contain all the vital background a reporter needs to write a story on your client.

If you are responsible for publicizing a large-scale activity, such as a rock concert or a major sporting event, there will be a central pressroom or press box. You should have an adequate stock of media kits in this room so that journalists can pick up whatever information they might need. This is also true at trade shows, where there is a central pressroom with media kits from all participating companies.

Typically, a media kit will contain the following:

- News releases describing whatever is being announced
- Biographies of any executives who will speak at the event
- Copies of any speeches delivered at the event
- A backgrounder or brochure on the company or individual sponsoring the event
- Photos and captions

Possible Questions from the Media and Draft of Answers

An important exercise in preparing for a news conference is to develop a list of questions that might come from the media. This list should be submitted to the people who will be speaking at the news conference so that they can prepare themselves for the media's questions.

To develop this list, research the subject of your announcement.

Ask any questions that are unanswered, or not completely answered, by the news release and speeches. And at every news conference you attend, take notes on the questions reporters ask. Doing so will help you anticipate questions in the future.

For your "Credit-Card TV" news conference, your executives might expect the following questions:

- When will the sets be available to consumers?
- Which retail stores will carry them?
- What kind of power source is needed for the product?
- What is the retail price structure for the sets?
- Will these sets be available in foreign markets?
- Are you aware of any other companies that might be introducing a similar product?
- What are your exptected first-year sales for these sets?
- How long did it take to develop this product?

These questions are typical of those asked during many product announcements.

As the public relations writer, you will also often be expected to develop the answers to these questions. In drafting your answers, you should follow the same procedures for research, writing, and approval outlined in Chapter 4.

On-site Arrangements

Entire books have been written on how to throw a good party or produce a successful event. Because this book focuses on writing, we will not delve into the countless details involved in coordinating the on-site activities of a large event. We will, however, offer an overview of the basic items you should keep in mind when planning an event:

- *Location.* Always plan ahead in selecting a site for a media event. Common sites, such as hotel banquet rooms, are often reserved at least two or three months in advance, especially during busy convention periods and holiday times. Try to book a site at least two months in advance and *always* visit the site before agreeing to host an event there. When selecting a site, keep in mind such factors as its reputation, the convenience of its location, room size, and accessibility for the media.

- *Menu* The menu is an important consideration. Depending on the type of event and who will be attending, you will be selecting either a very elegant, expensive menu or a simple coffee-and-Danish service. The food service is particularly significant at cocktail parties or festive galas.

- *Audiovisual equipment.* A broken slide projector can ruin a news conference. Always double-check your audiovisual equipment to make sure everything works, right up to the last minute before the event begins. Having backup equipment on hand is a good idea.

- It is important to make sure that the site of the event has adequate telephones and electrical outlets for your needs and those of the reporters. Electrical power is particularly critical during product demonstrations that require industrial outlets. Often you will have to arrange for electricians to be on-site, and this is an extra item for the budget.

- *Signage.* Place your client's name or logo in a prominent spot that will always be included in photographs or TV interviews. The most common spot to hang a sign is on the podium behind which the main speaker will be standing. It is also useful to hang banners behind the head table and to put large signs on the walls. Avoid using bright white backdrops, which are hard for television cameras to pick up.

- *Name badges.* It is helpful to have name badges for everyone attending and participating in a special event. Badges should be prepared *before* the event (use your participant and RSVP lists). Arrange the badges in alphabetical order at the sign-in desk for the event. Bring along extra blank badges for unexpected guests.

- *Sign-in book.* A sign-in book, or register, should be at the entrance to your event, and guests should be asked to enter their names and company or media affiliation. This book is invaluable for your follow-up work, since it contains the name of every journalist who attends the event.

Rehearsal

As discussed in Chapter 4, it's a good idea to hold a dress rehearsal of any presentation or event enough in advance to allow for any necessary refinements or changes. This means having the featured speakers read their speeches, testing out all of the audiovisual equipment, staging a mock question-and-answer session, and generally going over all the details of the upcoming event.

Often a rehearsal will uncover details that were overlooked during planning. Attending to them now will help ensure smooth sailing during the actual event.

The PR Newswire and the Businesswire

The PR Newswire and the Businesswire are wire services that run public relations announcements for a fee. Most major broadcast and print media have each of these newswires in their newsrooms and assign someone to monitor them.

In many cases, you will want to remind editors about your event by sending a message across these newswires on the morning of the event. And you may want to transmit the main news release describing your announcement across these newswires right after the news conference ends.

Often you will want to follow up an event by issuing a release summarizing it. This release will be in the past tense and include such information as the names of any notable individuals who attended, how many people attended in total, and how much money was spent or raised.

Follow-up

After the event is over, you will need to conduct a great deal of quick follow-up work with the media. This may include supplying photographs, setting up interviews, and sending out press kits to those who could not attend the event. You should always have extra press kits for purposes such as this.

You will also want to monitor the media coverage resulting from the event. Use your sign-in book to determine who attended the event, and watch those media outlets carefully to see if a story on your client does indeed appear.

The Press Junket

A press junket is a special tour for reporters and editors wherein transportation and accommodations are provided so that the journalists can view a particular event. In return, media coverage is expected (but, naturally, no attempt is made to influence the coverage one way or another).

For example, travel writers are often sent on press junkets to the opening of a new resort or to visit a tourist attraction. Many press members do not accept junkets, because they see them as compromising a journalist's objectivity and impartiality. Many freelance writers, however, do accept junkets, for access to particular stories.

Planning junkets is similar to planning other special events, though there are also many travel details to coordinate. Pitch letters are the main vehicle used for inviting press members on junkets.

The Publicity Tour

A publicity tour consists of scheduled publicity appearances in a series of cities. Publicity tours are most often used to publicize books, concert tours, or the introduction of a new product or service into local markets. They are also set up to take advantage of a celebrity's or top executive's travel schedule.

The planning and writing involved in a publicity tour are essentially the same as those in booking broadcast appearances or in setting up interviews for print media. (See Chapters 2 and 5 for discussions of the specific writing skills entailed.)

Chapter Recap

Special events are time-consuming, highly detailed activities that require a great deal of planning and organization. The most important part of a successful event is the planning. Always try to anticipate possible disasters so that you can avoid them or respond effectively. Murphy's Law, which states that anything that can go wrong will go wrong, aptly applies to special events.

In review, your checklist when preparing a special event should look like this:

- Invitation list—press and others
- Time and date: possible conflicts
- Invitations
- Media alert
- Photo opportunity alert

- Callbacks to invited press members to firm up attendance
- Daybooks
- Media kit
    Speeches
    Main announcement release
    Technology release
    Executive bios
    Company backgrounder/fact sheet
    Photos/captions
- Possible questions from the media and draft of answers
- On-site arrangements
    Room rental
    Menu
    Audiovisual equipment
    Electrical hookups
    Signage
    Name badges
    Sign-in books
- Rehearsal
- The PR Newswire and the Businesswire
- Follow-up

7

Business Writing

Expanding Your Readership

Business or financial writing forms a separate branch of public relations. Master it, and you will have access to a whole new realm of challenging, often better-paying jobs. The reason? Countless public relations people—able professionals, in many cases—cannot get the hang of the business side of corporate communications. If you can, your career opportunities are broadened considerably.

Business writing also brings you a whole new and avid readership: the business media and, through them, the investor community. Business audiences are less interested in being entertained than in being informed. They want information about your company, information that will guide their investments. What you write, therefore, can influence the value of your company's stock, the way the outside world judges your company's management, and possibly the perceived value of your company.

Financial writing also brings you yet another group of interested readers: the Securities and Exchange Commission (SEC), the federal agency that regulates the world of Wall Street. Most publicly owned companies must file a series of documents with the SEC each year and send to the commission copies of public reports and news releases that relate to the company's financial affairs.

Under these conditions, you have little room for embellishment and *no* room for mistakes. If what you write is inaccurate or misleading, your company may be liable for civil lawsuits and even criminal prosecution. As Carl W. Schneider and Jason M. Shargel put it in "Now That You Are Publicly Owned," a review of SEC obligations of public companies,

Press releases must avoid misstatements or material omissions. A high degree of accuracy, completeness and balance between positive and negative factors is required. There is no room for the degree of puffing in financial disclosures which would be acceptable in general commercial advertising or other areas of commercial communication.[1]

In other words, the creative liberties that might be acceptable in publicizing a rock star or a gallery opening would be unacceptable in announcing your company's financial performance.

The Basics: Vocabulary, Confidentiality, Style

If you plan to make a career in corporate communications of any kind—and especially in the investor relations area—you will need to learn at least the basic elements of business and develop a working knowledge of the field or industry in which you have chosen to apply your craft. This may be self-taught (it *can* be done) or acquired on the job (if you're lucky). But if you are still in school, or thinking about going back, give some thought to at least a semester or two of business courses. The knowledge has a way of coming in handy.

If you already understand these business principles, feel free to skip ahead in the chapter. But if you find yourself caught short, it may help to review the definitions of the basic vocabulary used in financial writing.

Vocabulary

Let's imagine you work for a medium-size corporation, MSC, Inc. MSC is a *publicly held* company, meaning it sells shares of itself—stock—to the public through a stock exchange or market. (Privately owned companies—sole proprietorships and partnerships—are not as legally obligated to announce their activities. They rarely issue public financial statements.)

---

[1]Carl W. Schneider and Jason M. Shargel, "Now That You Are Publicly Owned," *Business Lawyer* 36 (July 1981): 1631. © 1981 by the American Bar Association.

MSC takes in money (in the form of *income, revenues,* or *sales*) by selling its products or services. It deducts expenses of various kinds. Income minus expenses equals *profits* (*earnings,* or *net income,* which may be computed *pre-* or *posttax.* A certain amount of posttax profits will usually be paid to shareholders in the form of *dividends.* These should not be confused with *earnings per share,* which are simply profits divided by the total number of shares outstanding.

MSC is governed by a *board of directors,* whose members are elected by shareholders at MSC's *annual meeting* (which the company is legally bound to hold). Under the leadership of a board chairperson, the directors appoint the corporation's president and officers.

Because it is regulated by the SEC, MSC must make regular financial reports to the commission and the public. MSC must issue an annual report to shareholders, and it must generally announce any change or event within the corporation that might influence investors.

Like most corporations, MSC maintains a separate department—investor relations—for communicating with Wall Street and with the national and global financial community. For news releases and other announcements, investor relations people may work closely with the corporate information department.

Enter the financial writer. Your responsibility is to convey the facts, and MSC's point of view about the facts, as clearly and concisely as possible.

Confidentiality

MSC's obligation to make periodic public disclosures of its financial performance does not mean that *every* financial fact about your company must be made public. It is crucial, therefore, that you have a clear understanding of what your company wants to disclose and what it wants to keep confidential. For example, MSC may announce revenues and profits for each of its major operating areas but choose not to break out of these numbers for each subsidiary unit within those areas. The key for you and your department is to adopt a *well-defined policy* and stick to it.

You must also be very careful about how and when you disclose financial information. Wall Street has been rocked in recent years by a series of prosecutions for what is called "insider trading"—the use of information that has not been publicly disclosed to identify stocks that are about to skyrocket or plummet. In one of the most publicized cases, a reporter for the *Wall Street Journal* was found guilty of profiting from stock tips before they were published in his column.

The lesson of these cases for you as a corporate business writer is that whatever you disclose *must* be made available to everyone—financial analysts, newspapers, wire services—at the same time. If you give an advance look at a particular release to a favored reporter or investment analyst, you could be liable for a lawsuit or criminal charge.

Style

Business writing has a reputation for being pompous and boring that is generally well deserved. From convoluted syntax to clichéd football metaphors, much of the prose that comes out of corporate America reads like a "Don't" list for aspiring writers. As William Strunk, Jr., and E. B. White observe in *The Elements of Style*,

> The businessman says that ink erasers are *in short supply*, that he has *updated* the next shipment of these erasers, and that he will *finalize* his recommendation at the next meeting of the board. He is speaking a language that is familiar to him and dear to him. Its portentous nouns and verbs invest ordinary events with high adventure; the executive walks among ink erasers caparisoned like a knight. This we should be tolerant of—every man of spirit wants to ride a white horse. The only question is whether his vocabulary is helpful to ordinary prose. Usually, the same can be expressed less formidably, if one makes the effort.[2]

The problem with business jargon, Strunk and White go on to point out in their wonderful handbook, is that meanings change quickly (e.g., note how our usage of *update* has changed from "move up in time" to "bring up to date"), and that in any case,

[2]William Strunk, Jr., and E. B. White, *The Elements of Style* (New York: Macmillan, 1972), p. 68.

many people didn't understand what the words meant in the first place.

As a public relations business writer, you cannot correct this failing all by yourself. You can, however, turn it to your advantage. In the midst of all this cluttered writing, a clear, lean prose style can make your company look more astute and more professional than its competition.

For the reasons we've stated above, business and financial writing assignments offer far fewer opportunities for prose experiments than most other public relations writing assignments do. Don't waste time and energy looking for some offbeat approach; just get the facts down as plainly and understandably as you can. Successful business writing does not call attention to itself.

The Business Release

When something big happens—when your company buys or sells a major segment of its business, when it issues new shares of stock or buys back old ones, when it introduces a new product line—you are likely to issue a release. Here your headline and approach will be dictated by the event:

MSC ACQUIRES SMALL CORPORATION

or

MSC WINS GOVERNMENT CONTRACT

or

MSC DECLARES 17¢ DIVIDEND

The form of the release should be crisp and factual, with *what* followed by *why*. The explanation—the why—may come in the way of a quotation from your company president. A paragraph or two of background, perhaps on the company or on the industry as a whole, can then follow.

The Quarterly Report

As a public relations business writer, the most common writing assignment you will encounter is the news release announcing the corporation's performance at the end of each *quarter* (a three-month period in either the calender or the fiscal year). These releases begin with a brief statement of the company's revenues and pretax profits, with comparisons with the same period in the prior year. Similar breakdowns by operating division may follow.

Next, usually, come comments about the figures by the president or chairperson. Finally, the release details any noteworthy events from the quarter just completed. The news release also typically contains a chart or table of the financial results in numerical form.

Assuming that the fictional MSC, Inc. has three divisions— MSC/USA, MSC/International, and MSC Ventures—a sample quarterly release might look like this:

FOR RELEASE: April 5, 1993
CONTACT: Jane Smith, Vice-President,
Corporate Information
(202) 555–1234

MSC FIRST-QUARTER RESULTS IMPROVE ON 1992 PERFORMANCE

MSC, Inc.'s revenues and net income for the first quarter of 1993 were both ahead of the record totals for the same period last year, the company announced today. Results for the quarter just completed are as follows:

First Quarter	1993	1992	Change
Revenues	$378 million	$284 million	+33%
Net income	$ 25 million	$ 18 million	+39%
Net income per share	$ 1.42	$ 0.98	+45%

"Our first-quarter performance reflects the sharp improvement in domestic and international markets we've been experiencing since the third quarter of last year," said Joseph A. Medium, Chairman and Chief Executive Officer. "We are also seeing positive results from the cost-cutting programs we've implemented at all three of our operating divisions, and we expect to make further progress in this area as the year goes on."

For the three-month period that ended March 31, MSC/USA revenues rose 33 percent over 1992 first-quarter levels, while net income increased 49 percent. MSC/International's revenues and net income

improved by 25 percent and 19 percent, respectively, in part because of the weakening of the U.S. dollar as measured against foreign currencies. Revenues for MSC Ventures rose by 18 percent, but
net income declined 7 percent, primarily due to start-up costs for the
division's new compact-disc manufacturing operation.

The MSC Board of Directors today also announced a quarterly
dividend of 17¢ per fully diluted share of common stock.

As the year goes on, columns of figures comparing six-month, nine-
month, and year-to-year totals will be added as well. The year-end
summary, as you might expect, is the most detailed, and it serves as
a basis for the annual report.

Headlines and lead sentences in quarterly reports should meet the
same journalistic standards as those in other kinds of news releases.
They should always be clear and concise. If there is something to
highlight, highlight it:

MSC POSTS BEST-EVER FIRST-QUARTER RESULTS

or

SALES, EARNINGS UP AT MSC

or

MSC REVENUES RISE FOR NINTH CONSECUTIVE QUARTER

If, however, the news is not so good, you are under no obligation to
trumpet it. A common approach—and a perfectly acceptable one—
is this:

MSC REPORTS FIRST-QUARTER RESULTS

Some companies use that form even when the news is good. On the
other hand, avoid a headline like this:

MSC YEAR-END TOTALS ANNOUNCED

It sounds like the news is being dragged out of you. Stick to the
active voice.

You should expect to draft the quotation from your chief executive as well. This should be basic, straightforward, and explanatory.
Stick with simple sentences and active verbs.

After you've written a draft, your most important job begins: fact-checking. You could send out the most boring, hackneyed quarterly report in the history of finance, and probably not one investor or financial reporter would complain. But misstate a fact or, heaven forbid, add the numbers incorrectly, and the mail will pour in as though *New York Times* language columnist William Safire had made a grammatical error.

So add the numbers correctly. Use a calculator. Make sure the statements in the release have been cleared by the financial department or the legal department, or both. Remember, you are writing for highly skeptical readers. You want to present your corporation as the sound, savvy, responsible business it is. You have the ability—a much greater ability than you might suspect—to influence how Wall Street sees your company. Strict factual accuracy at *all times* is paramount.

The Annual Report

Once upon a time, annual reports chronicled the growth of American industry. Today, they have become a growth industry in themselves, with corporations striving to top the competition—and their own past efforts—in turning out reports that utilize some of the most beautiful examples of contemporary graphic design.

The finished product inevitably says a lot, in words and in pictures, about the company that creates it. For example, Sony projects a cool elegance in its approach and graphic design. Time Warner opts for a hot, daring look. H. J. Heinz offers a two-volume report in a handsome slipcover: Volume 1 contains the text; Volume 2, a beautiful photographic essay on the fifty-seven varieties and more.

Some shareholders complain that the money spent on these expensive productions would be better put into their dividends. For most investors, however, annual reports are a form of entertainment and a tangible symbol of the pride they feel in owning a piece of corporate America.

Your job, as the writer of your company's annual report, is to reinforce that pride. The report should project as positive and upbeat a picture as possible—without straying past the boundaries of accuracy and clarity as set forth by the SEC.

Setting a Timetable

Annual reports must be published on a strict schedule. By law, your company must hold an annual meeting that must be preceded (by more than a month) by the issuing of a proxy statement and a report to shareholders. If you are responsible for turning out your company's report, you *must* meet that deadline.

Your work starts, therefore, with the creation of a schedule that will ensure the report's timely release. Begin with that date and work backward, figuring in how long it will take your printer to print and bind the report, how long for your art director to assemble photos and illustrations and lay out the report, and how long for you to research and write the text. Build in *lots* of time—several weeks, at least—for securing approvals from management and making corrections and changes. No matter how brilliant and appropriate your prose, changes will be made. Count on them. Budget for them. If your company operates on a calendar year and you want to issue your annual report in March, the planning should begin in late summer or early fall, and the actual gathering of art materials should follow soon after. The writing itself should be well under way by December. (For more information on publications, see Chapter 8.)

What Goes In

By law, your annual report must contain a variety of financial statements (the preparation of which will probably be the responsibility of the financial department); a discussion of the state of your industry, the financial condition of your business, and the results of its operations in the past year; and a description of your company's structure and the businesses in which the company is engaged.

From a writer's standpoint, annual reports offer a chance not only for a longer, more developed piece of work, but also for a more flexible and interesting approach to style. Boring annual reports make a company look stodgy or worse. Good annual reports should read like a good business magazine, while projecting a confident, dynamic image for the company. You are writing for intelligent, knowledgeable readers. Don't insult them. Don't kid yourself into believing you can hide your company's problems (if there are any) behind verbal fluff.

A Sample Framework

In most cases, you'll want to put the numbers at the back. Many shareholders won't even read the financial statements, and in any case, it is the words and pictures, not the numbers, that generate the pride and positive feeling you are trying to foster. A page of financial "headlines" at the top makes a good introduction.

Here's a sample framework, with elaboration on items 2 and 3 given in the sections below:

1. Financial highlights
2. Chairperson's letter to shareholders (introduction)
3. Description of the business
4. Detailed look at operating areas
5. Introduction to the financial section
6. Financial statements

CHAIRPERSON'S LETTER. Think of your annual report as a long news article. Each of your readers is interested in the article to some degree. Some will read every word. Some will look only at the pictures. To please and inform as many of these people as possible, you'll want to organize the report so that it moves from the general to the particular; the more the shareholder reads, the more he or she will find out about the company's year. The ultimate details—the financial breakdowns—come last.

In this sort of framework, the chairperson's letter makes an ideal introduction. It should include an overview of each major area of business and commentary on the year just concluded. If the shareholder wants to read no further, he or she will at least have a good idea of what is going on at the company.

Unless your chairperson takes pride in an especially eccentric style (and there are more than a few such executives), the tone of the letter will be clear and businesslike. Since your readership includes the SEC, what you write about your business must accurately reflect what the numbers at the back of the report say.

Here's an example of a letter to the shareholders:

TO OUR SHAREHOLDERS

We remain extremely pleased with our company's continued strong performance in 1993. MSC's financial results—income from continuing operations, net income, and revenues—were at the highest levels in the company's history. Our investment in new and expanded product and service lines for the computer industry was also at an all-time high. We achieved this success by paying close attention to our customers and our costs and by improving the quality of our products and services.

Our largest business, MSC/USA, completed a year of substantial growth and greatly improved profitability. At a time when the domestic market for personal computers was experiencing little or no growth, MSC's longtime commitment to larger, mainframe computers for industrial or government use proved extremely fortuitous, and we are reinvesting heavily in research and development in this area.

MSC/International enjoyed another year of significant expansion in an ever-lengthening list of foreign territories. During the past twelve months, the division has opened subsidiaries in Spain, Portugal, Argentina, Peru, and Singapore, and discussions are under way for the creation of a cooperative venture between MSC and the People's Republic of China.

MSC continued its program of expansion into new business areas through the MSC Ventures division in the past year. Our local area network operations remain our fastest-growing business, and we look forward to continued steady growth in this area. Through MSC Ventures, the company has also entered the exciting new field of compact-disc mastering and manufacturing, our first entry into the computer applications of recorded music. In the fourth quarter, we broke ground on a compact-disc factory adjacent to our existing plant in Indianapolis, and we expect the new facility to be on-line by the first quarter of next year.

In closing, we want to share our feelings of pride and gratitude with all the MSC employees around the world who have contributed so much to our success. They deserve all our thanks, not only for what they have achieved, but also for the promise those achievements hold for our future.

[Signature]
Joseph A. Medium
Chairman and Chief Executive
Officer

DESCRIPTION OF THE BUSINESS. By law, the report must also include a description of the business, a concise summary of your corporation's structure (often illustrated by a chart), and the businesses in which the company is engaged. Keep it simple, direct, and factual. If you're writing more than, say, 300 words, either you work for a very large, very diversified company or you're overwriting. For MSC, the description could read like this:

THE MSC ORGANIZATION

MSC, Inc., is a diversified computer hardware and software company; employing more than 10,000 people worldwide in its principal businesses of computer hardware manufacturing, computer software design and marketing, local area networks, and compact-disc manufacturing. The company consists of three divisions: MSC/USA, MSC/International, and MSC Ventures. MSC is a leading designer of software for the educational and professional markets, domestically and around the world, as well as one of the top five U.S. manufacturers of mainframe computers. MSC Ventures operates a local area networks integration business, manufactures and markets computer accessories, and presses digital-audio compact discs for MSC's own software operation and for outside clients.

Business Presentations

Audiovisual presentations of financial and other business material are a way of life in the corporate world. Seldom are they fascinating. All too often, they are confusing, overly long, and poorly paced. Your goal as the writer and producer of a business presentation should be to put across the material as clearly and concisely as possible. Don't get carried away trying to enliven dull subject matter. Your audience will expect to be informed, not entertained, and they will be impressed by your presenter's grasp of the material, not by his or her sense of humor.

A Few Words about Taste

Because business presentations tend to be extremely dry, and because business (especially finance) has until recent years been almost exclusively run by men, business conferences and meetings have traditionally had the tone of a men's-club smoker, if not a stag party. Before you put together your first presentation for such a meeting, remember: Times have changed.

A colleague of ours recently endured a half-hour financial presentation put on by a division of a prominent U.S. corporation. The executives making the presentation apparently assumed that no one would be interested in the material they were presenting, and so they all but submerged it in the following:

- Ethnic jokes (a tortured and stale *Godfather* takeoff, complete with stereotypical accents)
- Sexist jokes (a slide of a woman in a bikini dropped in among a series of financial charts)
- Tasteless jokes (taking off on the Chernobyl nuclear disaster)
- Just plain stupid jokes (of the caliber of "Take a look at that asset")

The news here is not that the presentation was made this way. The news is that *no one laughed.*

Near the beginning, a few nervous chuckles came from the mostly male audience, but after only a minute or two, the listeners were squirming in their seats, more than they would have at the most boring parade of numbers. Afterward, the whole room was whispering about how bad the executives had made themselves look.

Humor can be useful tool. A little levity in the midst of a complicated presentation can be as welcome as a cold drink on a hot day. But before you insert *any* humor into your work, stop to ask yourself, "Is it appropriate? Is it in good taste?" And (last but not least) "Is it funny?" The downside risk, as they say in business, far outweighs the risk of being boring. When in doubt, leave it out.

The Script

Your text will look and read very much like a speech (see Chapter 4), with the addition of cues and references to any other media you are incorporating. Leave an extrawide margin on one side of each page, and insert cues where appropriate. Your finished copy will thus serve as a running script for your presenter(s), as well as a list of audiovisual and related cues for whoever is handling the technical side of the presentation. (If the media you are using are very complicated, you may want to prepare a separate technical outline.)

A Philosophy of Slides

Some people love slides. Their presentations—however brief, however seemingly simple—are awash in slides, carousel after carousel of them, slides to illustrate the most minuscule point or change of topic.

Slides have their place. They can simplify complex material, or instantly make clear something that would take much longer to explain in words. But just as a speech should be no longer than it has to be to cover the topic, slides should be used *only* when needed. Using slides to illustrate everything you say actually insults your listeners' intelligence; it's as if you were suggesting they couldn't understand the material any other way.

Coordination of Text and Slides

If every slide has a purpose, then logically your script must make that purpose clear. In other words, once you put a slide up on the screen, you have to talk about it in some way. Nothing confuses and exasperates an audience more than watching slides flash past while the speaker talks about something else entirely. It's hard enough following one line of thought without having to juggle two or more at the same time.

If a slide shows company revenues from 1988 to 1992, the text must in some way deal with that subject while the slide is on the screen. This doesn't mean you keep repeating "As you can see in our next slide" or similar phrases. Your presenter doesn't even need to look at the screen. (If the screen is directly behind the lectern, looking around will pull the presenter away from the microphone.) The slide belongs on the screen as long as it pertains to what is being said, after which the slide should come off immediately.

But don't make the mistake of going to the opposite extreme and reading every word and every number on every slide. Your audience can absorb images on the screen faster than you can recite the same information—that's the reason you're using slides in the first place.

Continuity

Once you begin a slide presentation, you must keep something on the screen at all times, until all the slides are finished. Raising and lowering the houselights again and again is clumsy, and the repeated transitions from light to dark can irritate the audience. If portions of your script need no slides, you can use slides of your company logo, or very general topic slides, as filler. Wherever possible, group your material so that you need few such filler slides. When your slides are finished, bring the lights back up. In the dark, people tend to fall asleep.

Putting It Together

Rehearse, rehearse, rehearse. There is a mysterious law of the universe that says any audiovisual machines or materials you fail to check before your presentation will fail to work when you need them.

Rehearsal also allows you to check on the flow of the presentation. Are the slides in order? Are they correctly placed in the projector? Are the slide cues in the right places in the script? Can your presenter see the script with the lights down? Does slide 1 appear while topic 1 is being discussed and disappear immediately after? Are videotapes rewound to the correct starting points?

Proofread the finished slides. Check the arithmetic. Unless you're making the presentation yourself, you can't be certain there will be no mistakes. What you *can* ensure is that the people doing the talking go in as well prepared as you can make them. A good presentation is like a successful play: The audience's response is immediate. Thorough preparation earns you your share of the credit.

Chapter Recap

In review, the steps for creating effective business and financial news releases are these:

- Follow the steps for producing media releases as outlined in Chapter 1.
- Learn basic financial vocabulary and use it correctly.
- Research thoroughly and recheck figures for accuracy.
- Write in a clear, direct style.
- Maintain confidentiality.
- Meet all timing and reporting requirements of the SEC.

Additionally, when writing annual reports, do the following:

- Set a timetable that will ensure meeting the deadline set by the SEC.
- Create a framework or outline that covers all the information required by the SEC and goes from an overview, to sections about the business, to the specifics of the financial results. For instance:

  Financial highlights
  Chairperson's letter to shareholders (introduction)
  Description of the business
  Detailed look at operating areas
  Introduction to the financial section
  Financial statements

- Work closely with the art director to fit copy and to ensure that the text and the visuals work together to enhance the company image.
- Allow ample time for several rounds of approvals and changes.

When scripting audiovisual business presentations, adopt these guidelines:

- Follow the principles of speech writing discussed in Chapter 4.
- Keep the material clear, concise, and in good taste.
- Create a script that shows the timing of each slide in relation to the text.
- Make sure there is a clear purpose for each slide.
- Keep a slide on the screen only as long as it is directly relevant to the text.

- Keep a slide on the screen at all times, until the slide portion of the presentation is complete, using as few logo or filler slides as possible.
- When the slides are finished, turn on the lights.
- Rehearse.
- Proofread slides and recheck the arithmetic.
- Recheck the audiovisual equipment and slides or tapes.

8

Publications

The Editorial Stage

The public relations agency or department is typically responsible for creating a varied spectrum of literature about the organization or client it represents. This may include product or promotional publications—often referred to as collateral advertising—annual and quarterly reports, and other in-house publications (those written and published by the company itself) aimed at employees, distributors, and key market and customer segments.

There is a wide range of choices for in-house publications, from a one-page newsletter to, say, a sixty-four-page, four-color magazine. A company's marketing goals may call for promotional brochures explaining how the company functions, the services it offers, or the products it manufacturers. Or a client may require an annual report to shareholders, material for fund-raising, program guides, or direct-mail solicitations. In-house publications are also used for internal purposes; an example is an employee newsletter that informs employees about projects and activities within the company.

The task of producing publications falls into two distinct categories, one editorial and the other production. Although no one can become an expert on publications without actually working on them, this chapter offers an overview of the specialized vocabulary and procedures involved in planning and writing sponsored publications. Unlike a contributor to a commercial publication that lists numerous people on its masthead, indicating a division of labor among many, the editor/writer of a corporate publication usually supervises all stages of planning and execution. Since this is a book on writing, this chapter focuses on the editorial side. Both traditional production and desktop and electronic publishing are covered in Appendix C.

Editorial Considerations

Begin the editorial process by asking yourself these "big picture" questions:

- What overall message do I want to communicate, and to whom? [It's important to know whom you're writing for and never to lose sight of this audience.]
- What information do I want to convey? What do I want to exclude? [Publications that try to cover too much ground are usually ineffective.]
- What image do I want to project?
- How do I combine these factors?

Then ask yourself these questions, which are more specific:

- What kind of editorial treatment will meet these goals? What are the features to be communicated [e.g., a new product or process, or a merger or expansion], and, more importantly, what are the potential benefits to the target audience?
- How many pages should the publication run, and what size format should it have? [Most publications are designed as multiples of four pages, because the majority of printing presses work most efficiently on that basis. Mailing considerations may influence your decision on the size and dimensions of the publication: The more the publication weighs, the costlier it is to mail; and an odd size or shape may not fit into any standard-size envelopes and thus require expensive, custom-made envelopes.]
- Should this be a one-time publication, a series, or a regularly issued newsletter?
- How much of the copy can I write, and how much should be assigned to others [freelance writers or others on your staff]?
- How will my editorial content be different from that of my

competitors' publications and commercial publications? What is the environment in which this piece must be positioned? Are there too many newsletters reaching this target audience already? Is this a "me-too" product, even though new for this company or client? If it is, what's better or distinctive about it?
- Who needs to approve the editorial plan before I begin implementing it?

By now, the theme of getting approvals before you proceed on projects should be familiar. Find out who must review your ideas, and present them clearly and concisely. It's advisable to offer editorial proposals (in writing or at meetings) with more ideas than one publication can actually contain. That way, you are prepared with alternatives to ideas that are rejected. Most people like choices, and the more you give them, the better the chance for speedy approvals. If and when your idea is rejected, don't be defensive or take the rejection personally. Be professional and eager to please. Remember, it's your client's publication, and your client has to be happy with it. Your role is to suggest ideas and formats and oversee them to completion.

To help decide on the specific editorial content of your publication, always put yourself in the role of the typical reader you are addressing. Ask yourself: "If I were a member of this organization, [or an employee of this corporation, a customer of this business, or a constituent of this official], what would I want and need to know? What would be helpful and informative to me? What would convince me to think [or plan, buy, or vote] a certain way?" Your answers to these questions will lead you to useful editorial ideas.

Very often, you will be able to draw on existing material from your public relations files and use it as background for your publications. For instance, a speech given by your client could, with a little alteration, become an editorial column in a magazine. A series of advertisements could provide a basis for a sales promotion brochure or a persuasive article. A series of press releases could be adapted as newsletter items. Be aware of all of your client's activities and of the resources available. Good research is an essential prerequisite to writing and producing effective publications.

Newsletters

Internal Newsletters

Larger companies often circulate newsletters internally to employees on both management and lower staff levels. Items such as promotions, department changes, retiree news, informational quizzes, department features, marriages, births, and even the results of company sports team competitions may be included. Internal newsletters also apprise the rank and file of policy changes, company outlook, different departments' priorities, company benefits, and so forth. Often they will carry messages from the president, and they are an excellent forum for letting employees know what is going on in areas outside their immediate sphere.

In large corporations with locations throughout the country, it is becoming increasingly common to produce employee "newsletters" in video form. Essentially, the editorial challenge remains unchanged, and the copy becomes a series of scripts. Some companies may also deliver internal news via computer.

When writing any "internal" publication, keep in mind that it might be read by people external to the company, including members of the media.

External Newsletters

Newsletters are also used to inform audiences outside the company, such as the media, members of a particular industry, dealers, distributors, suppliers, and securities analysts, to name just a few. The editorial content of a newsletter varies with each client. If you are writing one for IBM, for example, you might focus on new products or on sales of existing lines. You might also report on interesting trends in a certain division, new technology applications, or significant research results.

But if you're producing a newsletter for a prominent rock-and-roll artist, you will, of course, craft the newsletter in an entirely different way. You might report on new recordings due for release, itineraries of upcoming concert tours, or recent awards received or distinctions achieved. In many cases, topics of general interest to the industry are discussed, with a slant toward how your client is involved or affected.

For every client, you must analyze the composition of your audience and decide what information will both fulfill your client's objectives and interest your readers.

Corporate Brochures

Corporate brochures are key items in sales, promotion, and media kits. The brochure is normally a presentation of the company's distinctive capabilities, as they apply to the corporation as a whole, an operating division, or a single product line. The form—use of four-color photography, art, or illustrations, or choice of design or paper stock—is dictated by the content. A style appropriate to consumer products, for example, might appear too frivolous for financial products, which might require a more straightforward style.

The corporate brochure presents information about a client and usually covers these areas:

- Who we are
- Where we come from (background on company)
- What we offer (service, product)
- How or where we are available
- Why we're special

From the outset, it's critical to identify the key messages in terms of features and benefits. Features are the nuts-and-bolts of a company or product; benefits describe what's in it for the reader.

The length of the corporate brochure will be determined by the messages the client wants to communicate, the budget, and how often the brochure will be updated: Brevity is unfailingly a virtue. The most effective brochures are almost invariably those which succeed in communicating their key messages with the greatest economy of words. The life expectancy of a brochure—or its shelf life—is an important planning consideration.

Assigning Stories

Once you've received approvals for the editorial content of the publication, you may need to assign some of the copy tasks to other members of the public relations team or to outside writers. For a variety of reasons (discussed in other chapters), it is always important to know which reporters cover your industry. For your in-house publication, you may want to solicit copy contributions from reporters at trade and consumer publications that cover your field. Some reporters are allowed to accept outside assignments.

It's wise to build contacts with several competent freelance writers and to use good ones regularly. Such practices enable writers to learn how best to work with you and to gain some knowledge of the operations and communications needs of the clients you serve. List your choices of two or three writers for each article to be assigned. Call your first choice and ask if he or she is interested in a freelance assignment, and briefly describe the nature of the article, the fee, and the deadline.

Establishing Editorial Guidelines

Whether you plan to write copy yourself or assign it to another writer, the first task is to compile a body of source material that can be used as a starting point in developing the piece. The second task is to frame a general outline to serve as an editorial guideline for the writing.

The more specific your plans at the outset, the more likely is the resulting draft to be on target. It is easier to write a first draft in a disciplined manner than to rewrite an unsuccessful effort. Here are the key elements in an outline (or treatment):

- *A statement of the nature and focus of the article.* Never be vague. When appropriate, suggest people to be interviewed.
- *A statement of the article's length and deadline.*
- *A sampler of similar articles that serve as good models of what you are seeking.*

If you are assigning the piece to an outside writer, you'll also want to compose a letter commissioning the assignment. Also enclose background information about the company, and background information you have about the topic, and sample articles of the kind you expect from the commissioned writer. Following is a sample letter of commission:

Dear _____,

This letter confirms our conversation commissioning you to write an article for [title of publication] or [subject] . Your article should cover [subject] with particular attention devoted to [focus].

The article should run between [number] and [number] words, or approximately [number] double-spaced, typewritten pages. I'd like you to interview the following people for the article: [names, titles, and phone numbers].

The deadline for the piece is [date], and on acceptance we will pay you $[amount] for all worldwide publication rights for the article. We reserve the right to reject the article or request revisions if it does not meet with our editorial standards. If we must reject the article, the kill fee will be $ [amount] .

I've attached a few samples of similar articles we've published that might be helpful to you. Also attached is some background information about our company and some material related to your topic.

Please feel free to call me for any reason. I'll be happy to answer any questions you might have, or assist in any way. I'm delighted you are available to contribute to our publication, and I look forward to working with you.

Sincerely,

[Name, title]

Letters of commission will vary according to the writers and the assignments. If you are working with an experienced writer, you may want to leave out the rejection clause. Most of the time, it's a good idea to build into your editorial deadlines room for rewriting the piece or for reassigning it should the writer not deliver what you need. In other words, don't assume the article will be submitted in perfect shape. You must allow adequate time for editing.

Other Concerns: Format, Timeliness, Style Sheets

Format

You will have many editorial formats to choose among for your publication. Familiarize yourself with what your client has published before and liked or disliked. Always be aware of what your competitors produce, and take notes on what you may want to imitate.

Timeliness

Copy should usually be written in a way that does not make it timebound. You may be writing copy that will not be published for several months, or that must remain accurate for months or years to come. Production is a major expense, and brochures, in particular, may require a fairly long shelf life to be cost-effective.

Here's an example of how to free copy from a time frame: Instead of writing, "Five years ago, George Bush was elected president of the United States," you could write, "In 1988, George Bush was elected president of the United States." Of if you're writing about a company's product line, you might write, "The company's products *include* X, Y, and Z," instead of "The company's products *are* X, Y, and Z." That way, the copy will be accurate even if new products are added after your publication is printed.

Style Sheets

Use a style sheet or a stylebook to ensure consistency in spelling, abbreviation, punctuation, and so on. Some editors create their own style sheets, but most use the *AP Style Book* or *The New York Times Style Book*.[1]

Production

When all your copy has been written, edited, and approved, you are ready to move into production, the second phase of in-house publication. As noted earlier, both traditional production and desktop and electronic publishing are covered in Appendix C.

---

[1]Both books can be found in bookstores. Or you can order them directly by sending a purchase order to *AP Style Book*, Associated Press News Feature Department, 50 Rockefeller Plaza, New York, NY 10020 (telephone [212] 621–1500), and to *The New York Times Style Book*, c/o Random House, Westminster, MD 21157, Attention: Order Department (telephone [800] 638–6460).

Chapter Recap

The field of in-house publications is indeed a challenging area to work in, allowing many roles to be played—reporter, editor, and production manager.

In summary, here are some guidelines for the editorial stage of in-house publications:

- In planning a publication, decide what you want to communicate, who your audience or audiences will be, what image you want to convey, what kind of editorial treatment will achieve your goals, what size the publication will be, how often it will appear, how it will be different from your competitors' publications, and who needs to approve your editorial plan before you begin implementing it.

- When you have decided on your editorial guidelines, make writing assignments that state the nature and focus of the article, the people to be interviewed, the article's length, and the deadline. If you're using an outside writer, send him or her a letter of commission, attaching background material about the company and the topic, as well as samples of the kind of article you expect.

- Check everything twice—you can never be too careful. Verify information in a manuscript; whenever possible, have professional copyeditors check the manuscript before it is typeset. Verify photo captions. Assume nothing is correct until you get corroboration from reliable sources.

- Get approvals for everything. That applies to copy, art, and layout.

- Keep organized files. Save the original of copy that has initials of approval on it; save research files that have sources for information cited in copy; and so forth.

- Plan an editorial and production schedule that allows adequate time for each stage to be completed properly.

9

Responsive Writing

Setting the Record Straight

Most writing for public relations concentrates on positive news, such as product introductions, concert tours, factory openings, increased sales, and countless other items that serve as focal points for press releases and pitch letters. But what happens when something goes wrong? Or if your company or client is overlooked or ignored? Do the same writing rules apply? Is the writing style different?

There are various forms of responsive writing for problematic situations. These situations can range from a large-scale disaster, such as a plane crash that kills several hundred people, to a relatively minor problem, such as an executive being misquoted in a newspaper article.

Some of the more common forms of responsive writing are the following:

- Letters to the editor
- Official statements
- Crisis releases
- Guest editorials

Letters to the Editor

The letter to the editor of a newspaper or magazine is probably the most frequently used form of responsive writing. In many cases, these letters are simple notes of praise for a story well done or a congratulatory note on an interesting article—both of which can serve to bring an issue back into the spotlight. In addition, there are letters written in response to a negative or inaccurate statement about your client.

When a negative, incorrect, or unbalanced article about your client is published, you, as public relations writer, are often asked to draft a letter to the editor that either corrects inaccuracies in the article or points out positive elements of a story that were omitted. In this chapter, we will review several types of responsive letters, as well as discuss situations in which no response is the best course of action.

Letters Correcting Mistakes

News articles are occasionally published with incorrect facts. Sometimes the mistakes are minor, but they can be damaging nonetheless. When this happens to a client of yours, you should request a correction by phone, send a letter of correction to the editor, or do both. (The broadcast equivalent of a letter to the editor is an editorial reply, wherein local stations invite listeners or viewers to respond to issues discussed on the air. Guidelines for broadcast writing can be found in Chapter 5.)

The usual letter of correction to the editor responds to an error in the article. Imagine that a newspaper prints a story on your client, X&Z Industries, and reports that X&Z Industries—which recorded annual sales last year of $50 million—had annual sales last year of only $5 million.

Clearly, a $45 million mistake needs correcting. First you should find out whether the paper prints a regular corrections column, and if so, the name of the editor to whom you should address your submission. If a corrections column is not published, you should write a letter to the editor for the regular letters column. In many cases, you will be drafting the letter for either your client or your supervisor to sign.

Your letter of correction should usually include the following elements:

- The date and page on which the incorrect article appeared
- The incorrect information that was printed
- The correct information that should have been stated
- The name and title of the author of the letter

Thus, your letter on behalf of X&Z industries might look like this:

May 3, 1993

Mr. John Doe
Editor
Hometown Daily
111 Elm Street
Pleasantville, MO 63332

Dear Mr. Doe:

In your October 28 issue, an article appeared on page 17 that incorrectly stated annual revenues for X&Z Industries at $5 million.

Last year, X&Z Industries recorded revenues of $50 million, an increase of 20 percent over the previous year's total. We would appreciate your printing a correction stating our actual annual revenues.

Thank you very much for your attention to this matter.

Sincerely.

James Doe
President
X&Z Industries

To avoid confusion, it is sometimes more prudent not to mention the incorrect information that was originally printed. Your decision on whether to include these errors will depend on the severity of the situation and how it affects your client. In many cases, publications have a policy of printing only the corrected figures, without mentioning the original error.

Letters of Correction as Publicity Tools

Letters to the editor also present excellent opportunities for publicity.

The following sample letters to the editor carried by *Time* magazine not only correct misinformation, but generate publicity for the authors. The first is about a mention of Myers's Rum, and the other is a response to a story about the emergence of Cable News Network (CNN) as a first source of news:

A Rum Thing. I'm afraid your highly informative piece on the vitality of the cruise industry [Business, Feb. 17] tumbled overboard in identifying one of the ingredients of the drink Bahama Mama, which is served aboard some ships. You said it includes 151-proof Myers's rum. Seagram has been making Myers's rum for decades, and does not produce any with that high an alcohol content. Our standard for rum is 80 proof (or 40% alcohol). We're happy to leave to someone else whatever glory attaches to a rum that is more than 75% alcohol.

Jerome S. Mann, President
The House of Seagram
New York City[1]

You say, "Once upon a time, newspapers broke the news to the public. Then TV took over that role." The fact is, studies show that the majority of people say the first source of their news is radio. The most recent numbers from one consumer research survey showed radio at 48% and television at 30%.

Tom Martz, Executive Vice President
Northern California Broadcasters Association
San Francisco[2]

Each of these letters is short and clear; and each contains the full name and title of the author.

Letters Criticizing a Reporter's Conclusions

More complex are letters to the editor that take exception to a reporter's conclusions or implications about a client's personality, integrity, or professional standing. For example, an article that reports on the mismanagement of a company or a personal scandal often angers a client to the degree that he or she demands a scorching response be submitted for publication.

When drafting such response letters, keep in mind the following guidelines:

- Support your points of contention with facts. Do not use emotional responses to defend your position.
- Keep your letter brief.
- Try not to bring in lawyers or threaten to pull advertising from the publication.

[1]*Time*, March 23, 1992.
[2]*Time*, January 27, 1992.

- Make your opinion clear and easily understood.
- State your case professionally and *tactfully*. There is no need for the tone of your letter to be accusatory, derogatory, or in any other way inflammatory.
- Maintain good relations with the media. Don't anger or alienate reporters with vitriolic and overly critical letters.

Following are examples of letters to the editor that take exception to published articles. Almost all the letters are short, emphasize one or two very strong points, and use hard facts to back up claims.

The first letter, which appeared in *Time*, is from the Polish embassy's press attaché:

DAY OF INFAMY

In the section on the war in Europe, you wrote about the "methodical extermination of millions in the six Polish death camps." These were not Polish camps but Nazi ones. Millions of Jews, Poles, Russians and many other nationalities were slaughtered in the concentration camps built by German Nazis in locations that suited their theories of preparing "living space." For the benefit of the young, and in memory of those who died, such misleading references should be avoided.

Boguslaw M. Majewski,
Press Attaché
Embassy of Poland
Washington[3]

The letter is brief, refers directly to the original article, and states its point clearly.

In the next case, one article provoked letters from representatives of two rival newspapers, both disagreeing with what they felt were unfair assessments of their papers.

CALIFORNIA PAPER WAR

I agree completely with Martha Smilgis' description of the San Francisco *Chronicle* ("comical") as a "clubhouse newspaper" [Special Issue, Nov. 18]. I also agree with her characterization of the San

[3]*Time,* December 23, 1991.

Francisco *Examiner* as a paper that writes stories about the "scandalous activities of local politicians." What I don't understand is her judgment that this means the *Examiner* is "hardly better" than the *Chronicle*. What does she think newspapers are supposed to do if not report on scandalous activities of local politicians? It would be a violation of our public trust if we didn't. Sure, the L.A. *Times* is a great newspaper. But Los Angeles is not a real city. That's why the *Times* can afford to tell its readers a lot more about deforestation in Poland than about what's going on in their own mega-metropolis.

Phil Bronstein, Executive Editor
San Francisco Examiner
San Francisco

Smilgis' cheap shot at the San Francisco *Chronicle* should not go unchallenged. Besides Herb Caen, our staff includes a recent Pulitzer Prize winner and a reporter whose Persian Gulf war reports drew national attention. Our stories are carried on the *New York Times* news wire and our scoops sometimes make the national papers. Like a good bottle of California wine, the *Chronicle* is getting better with age.

Jeff Pelline, Business Writer
San Francisco Chronicle
San Francisco[4]

The writer of the second letter supports his position with a simile, as well as with facts.

When Not to Respond to a Critical Article

Writing a critical letter to the editor is delicate. There are times when it is in your best interest *not* to respond to a negative article with a letter to the editor. For example, if a particularly unpleasant incident is accurately reported about your client in an article, a letter to the editor would serve only to generate additional negative publicity about the incident.

You should be very careful when responding to negative news with a letter to the editor. For example, in its June 1991 issue, *Consumer Reports* published an article on long-term-care insurance that

[4]*Time,* December 16, 1991.

was highly critical of the industry. In response to the article, Carl J. Schramm, president of the Health Insurance Association of America, a trade organization, wrote a letter to the editor that appeared in a subsequent issue of the magazine.

Following is a copy of Schramm's letter. Note that it begins with dramatic charges that the article was "sensational, misleading, and lacked credibility." The letter goes on to accuse *Consumer Reports* of bias, "given [the magazine's] own repeated declarations that a total government solution to this problem is needed."

LONG-TERM-CARE INSURANCE

Your assessment of long-term-care insurance policies was sensational, misleading, and lacked credibility, given your own repeated declarations that a total government solution to this problem is needed. In the end, you have created needless confusion and fear among your readers, especially those who currently own such policies. Contrary to the implications in the article, there are solid, affordable products on the market right now. For example, policies sold by 12 companies representing 75 percent of the market exceed the benefit standards required by the National Association of Insurance Commissioners. If market abuses exist, they are not the result of lack of regulation—all but one state have specific laws governing long-term-care insurance. Enforcement of these laws, however, is equally critical.

Carl J. Schramm, President
Health Insurance Association of America
Washington, D.C.[5]

Unfortunately, this letter backfired for the Health Insurance Association of America. *Consumer Reports* published the following response:

The National Association of Insurance Commissioners' model law and regulation is weak and incomplete, and even its provisions haven't all been passed by every state. Confusion abounds in the marketplace. Terms and definitions are not standardized. None of the states protect consumers adequately against inflation, increases

[5]*Consumer Reports*, September 1991.

in premiums, or misrepresentations on the part of agents. And none assure a refund if the policy is dropped.[6]

As you can see, *Consumer Reports* responded with a factual defense of its article that is as damaging as the original article. Thus, the letter to the editor was detrimental to the insurance industry in the following ways:

- Consumers are again warned away from *all* of the policies offered by the long-term-care insurance industry, because no state laws protect them against inflation or increases in premiums.
- Consumers are warned about "misrepresentations on the part of agents," which could apply to any purchase of insurance.
- Consumers are told that no state ensures they will get a refund if the policy is dropped.
- Consumers are again warned that understanding insurance policies is complicated, because terms and definitions may not be standard.
- The National Association of Insurance Commissioners is criticized for having created a model law and regulations that are weak and incomplete, and have not been passed into law in every state.

Letters Requesting Publicity When a Client Has Been Left Out

In addition to correcting and responding to negative articles, letters to the editors are also written when mention of a company, product, client, or point of view on an issue is left out of an article. This type of letter is frequently used as a publicity tool.

Here are two examples of letters that are positive in tone, one to *Time* in response to an article on reforming the health care system in America and one to *Newsweek*. Both seize the opportunity to promote previously neglected parties:

My own legislation, the Universal Health Care for All Americans Act, would guarantee affordable, comprehensive health coverage to

[6]*Consumer Reports*, September 1991.

all. You ignored one of the most pressing concerns of the health-care debate: access to long-term care. When a catastrophic illness strikes, all Americans are vulnerable, especially senior citizens on fixed incomes. The average annual cost of staying in a decent nursing home is $30,000. After only 13 weeks in a nursing home, 7 in 10 elderly people who had been living alone will find their income reduced to the poverty level. Let us be aware that in addition to coverage for acute care, Americans need access to affordable long-term care.

Mary Rose Oakar, U.S. Representative
20th District, Ohio
Washington[7]

SOUTH DAKOTA'S SCHOLAR

In listing members of the U.S. Senate who are Rhodes scholars ("Clinton's Rhodes Brain Trust," National Affairs, May 4), you somehow neglected to include South Dakota's Sen. Larry Pressler, a Rhodes scholar of about the same vintage as Bill Clinton. Sen. Pressler attended Oxford University on scholarship during 1964–1965.

Kristi Sommers,
Communications Director
to Senator Pressler
Washington, D.C.
Editor's note: Newsweek regrets the omission.[8]

Congratulatory Letters

Finally, there are simple congratulatory letters to the editor, which can be used as vehicles for promoting yourself or your client. In each of the following two letters, the author praises *Time*, while promoting himself and his company or institution.

THE COLLEGE CRUNCH

I found your articles on the financial problems facing colleges and universities [Education, April 13] very insightful and thought provoking. One difficulty for students and their parents is the shock to the

[7]*Time*, December 16, 1991.
[8]*Newsweek*, May 25, 1992.

pocketbook when tuition rates are announced each year. For the past three years, Pacific University has used an innovative "tuition contract" tied to the consumer price index. Any increase in tuition rates for returning students is limited to the CPI for the calendar year preceding the annual setting of tuition rates. Such a guarantee comes at a cost. But we believe it shows concern for students' resources and an awareness that, fiscally, higher education must be increasingly innovative and resourceful or price itself out of the reach of the vast majority of Americans.

Donald S. Rushmer,
Vice President for Academic Affairs
and Provost
Pacific University
Forest Grove, Ore.[9]

The redesign of TIME Magazine is wonderful. You did it right. I am a publication designer, and I found myself turning each page of the "new" TIME without once being let down. The magazine not only has developed a distinctive look for itself but also is, for the moment, on the cutting edge of publication design for efforts of its size.

William Castronuovo, President
Castronuovo & Associates, Design
Boston[10]

Official Statements

An official statement is developed for crisis situations or controversial topics about which your client's views must be summarized and presented clearly in one standard or official comment. There are several reasons for developing an official statement. For example, if a company or an individual is involved in a lawsuit, it is extremely important to keep tight control over what is said to the press. This is particularly true in large organizations with several thousand employees, all of whom represent a company viewpoint.

Official statements are often drafted and sent to all top executives involved in the issues at hand to make sure the company viewpoint is understood and adhered to by everyone.

[9]*Time,* May 4, 1992.
[10]*Time,* May 11, 1992.

For example, if twenty-five people were killed in an explosion at one of the factories of X&Z Industries, an official statement from X&Z should be drafted to explain the company's perspective on the tragedy. That statement would then be used as follows:

- Company spokespersons would use it in radio and television interviews.
- News releases issued on the explosion would be written using the official statement as a guideline.
- Company editorials or letters to the editor about the incident would stick to the points outlined in the official statement.

The official statement should be developed by top management and public relations executives with the advice and approval of legal counsel. In addition to minimizing confusion, these statements are often used to protect a company or individual from saying the wrong thing or straying from the issues at hand.

Let's assume you are the public relations representative for Johnny Amp, a rock star who has just been arrested for cocaine possession. Your official statement to the press might look like this:

> Official Statement regarding Johnny Amp
> Because this matter is currently under legal proceedings, we cannot comment at this time.

This is an example of a very short, simple official statement in response to questions about a matter that your client would prefer not to comment on. The basic purpose of this statement is to let all members of the Johnny Amp entourage know that they should not comment to the press.

Oftentimes, however, you will want to use your official statement to further your client's views of the controversy at hand. For example, when responding to questions about the Palestine Liberation Organization's (PLO's) condoning acts of terrorism, Yasir Arafat, the chairman of the PLO, read the following official statement, excerpted in the *New York Times:*[11]

---

[11]"PLO Chairman Yasir Arafat," *New York Times,* November 8, 1985.

The P.L.O. denounces and condemns all terrorist acts, whether those involving countries or by persons or groups, against unarmed innocent civilians in any place. . . . The P.L.O. as of today will take all punitive measures against violators.

In the same article, Arafat's statement went on to say:

The P.L.O. reiterates the right of the Palestinian people to fight against the Israeli occupation in all possible ways; with the aim of withdrawal of the Israelis from these lands.

In his statement, Arafat makes quite clear where the PLO stands on terrorism and on the State of Israel.

While official statements can range from simple acknowledgments to complex dissertations, there are some common elements to keep in mind:

- Official statements are best used to control the message your client is communicating on a sensitive or complicated issue.
- Statements should always be approved by top management and legal counsel.
- Statements should be distributed internally to anyone who might be contacted by the media.
- To help executives with media clearance, a Q&A can also be circulated, listing probable specific questions and suggested or approved answers. (See Chapter 1 for guidelines on constructing a Q&A.)

Crisis Releases

When a crisis as dramatic as an earthquake or airline crash occurs, getting information to the media swiftly is essential. Timely and frequent status reports help control false rumors and ensure an accurate flow of facts as they become available; such reports also help officials avoid having to respond to questions with a "No comment." It is always advisable to assemble a crisis information team that has direct access to top company officials or the highest authorities involved.

Much of the writing involved in crisis situations conforms to the principles and formats already discussed in this and other chapters; however, they are worth reviewing in this context, and there are some additional points of form and style to keep in mind for crisis releases:

- Gauge the scope of interest your crisis is likely to attract. Is your story local, regional, national, or international? Assessing the range of interest will help you decide how much you will need to explain.
- Use bullets in writing the facts to make it easy for reporters to extract key information quickly.
- Release all information on official letterhead.
- Put a date and time on top of every page.
- Include the name and telephone number of a person who can be contacted twenty-four hours a day.
- Double- or triple-space the information in the release.
- Consult with legal counsel before releasing information.

Here is a sample statement issued immediately after an explosion at an industrial refinery in El Segundo, California:

[COMPANY LETTERHEAD]

Date: March 2, 1993
Time: 12:30 P.M.
Issued by: John Doe (202) 555–1234 (24 hrs.)

Explosion, unknown cause, at 12:01 P.M. at main refinery, 122345 Pacific Coast Highway, El Segundo.

- Two killed, fifteen injured.
- Injured taken to Lomita Catholic Hospital, 345567 Main Street, Lomita [phone number].
- Damage assessment of refinery in early stages.
- Company Information Center established at main entrance, refinery; (202) 555–1234.
- Rumor Control Center established at Main Office Building; public information line: (800) 555–1234.
- Fire under control at 12:25 P.M.

- Company fire teams assisted by El Segundo Fire Department (three engine companies, fourteen fire fighters). Company personnel involved: twenty-one fire fighters; numerous other employees assisting.
- *Note:* Except for Rumor Control line, all phone numbers for media use only.
- Company CEO will be available for statements and questions as soon as possible at Information Center. Exact time of briefing to be announced as soon as possible.

Minimizing Negative Reports

Additional elements to consider when faced with public relations crisis management include the following:

- Television news broadcasts need videotape and/or live reports from the scene to bring a story to life. If they have nothing else, they will rerun shots of the disaster over and over each time they update the report. Make sure that your company's point of view and positive efforts are covered by providing press opportunities and/or a videotaped statement by a spokesperson (e.g., the CEO, the head of corporate communications, or the chief safety officer).
- For radio, release an audiotaped statement by a company spokesperson.
- Prepare press kits that include background information a reporter can use to put the current incident into context. For example, for an airplane crash, such background material might cite government studies on the low ratio of accidents per passenger-mile, compared with that of automobile travel.
- Keep a log of what information was released, when, and to whom.
- Consider the use of answering-machine messages and a priority answering system to handle phone inquiries.
- Design a standard procedure for quick responses, news conferences, and regularly scheduled briefings (see Chapter 6 for information about arranging special events).

Anticipating a Crisis

Most companies face the possibility of a crisis, so anticipate your needs *before* a disaster strikes by trying to answer the following ten questions:

1. Does your company have a crisis response plan?
2. Does the plan have clear guidance from company executives and legal counsel?
3. Are the company's vulnerabilities outlined?
4. Do you have all available background information on hand?
5. Does the plan provide for a crisis management team?
6. Does the plan provide for rumor control?
7. Does the company have a crisis information center, complete with a rumor control set up, interview areas, and information management teams?
8. Do you have prepared, fill-in-the-blanks new releases for the media, the public, and the employees?
9. Do you have a list of home phone numbers for all key people, plus a companywide phone list?
10. Have plans been made to address media access to company property, and have provisions been made for buses and escorts?

Guest Editorials

Almost all major newspapers and magazines have an editorial page devoted to articles and letters expressing personal viewpoints on a wide variety of issues. These editorial pages usually contain one section in which the opinions of the publication are printed, and another in which readers express their views.

These sections, frequently called op-ed pages (for "opposite editorials"), are often seen by public relations executives as valuable and influential publicity opportunities. These op-ed pages may accept letters to the editor, articles with bylines, or editorial statements, all of which are referred to as editorials.

Getting your editorials published is difficult, particularly in large newspapers and magazines. Competition is stiff: the *New York Times* receives numerous submissions for its op-ed page every day, but uses only two or three. The *Chicago Sun-Times* receives four to five per day, but prints only six per week, while *Newsweek* receives 150 or more submissions per week for the one opportunity to be published in its "My Turn" column.

There is no strict method for writing an editorial. Writing styles vary, from colloquial to academic. There are, however, some general guidelines to follow when preparing an editorial:

- Submit a brief essay. The average length of an editorial is three to five double-spaced, typewritten pages, or approximately 500 to 800 words.
- Choose a timely topic. The essay must be newsworthy and of current interest. Typical subjects include pending legislation; political, social, or economic controversy; recent disasters; changes in government; and new ordinances.
- Present a strong point of view. Because space is limited, your point must be made clearly and emphatically. Your opinion should be crystal-clear to the reader.
- Offer a prestigious authority. Being famous or being a leader in your field helps. For example, it is much easier for Lee Iacocca, the chairman of Chrysler Corporation, to have his article accepted for publication than it is for an average citizen.
- An editorial usually requires an in-depth and passionate viewpoint on a particular subject. In most cases, you will be ghostwriting for a top executive, and it is essential to interview that executive before drafting the editorial.

"Editorials are only successful when you're dealing directly with the top guy, or with only one layer of management at the most," says Richard Blodgett, a freelance writer and former reporter for the *Wall Street Journal* and *Business Week*. Blodgett, who has written numerous editorials, primarily for corporate executives, believes in basing his pieces on one or two solid ideas and backing them up with incisive, revealing facts.

"There's a premium on stating your viewpoint right up front," Blodgett says. "A few key facts are very good, but don't go overboard. One or two convincing facts are great, but any more can dilute the overall effect." In addition, Blodgett believes that passion and insight are the keys to good editorials.

The following editorial "Litigation Journalism is a Scourge" from the *New York Times* (Feb. 15, 1993) was written by Carole Gorney, a journalism professor and director of the public relations curriculum at Lehigh University. Her article makes a strong case against plaintiff's attorney using the media to influence litigation:

BETHLEHEM, Pa.

Litigation blackmail is being committed in the United States every day, aided and abetted by journalists, lawyers and public relations consultants. In a practice euphemistically called litigation journalism, lawyers are hiring public relations consultants to schedule talk-show appearances and newspaper interviews for their clients in an obvious attempt to generate public sympathy and apply pressure on the defendants.

While NBC's video of a staged crash of a G.M. truck would seem to be an outrageous example of litigation journalism, the episode was in most ways atypical. The drama may have been doctored by tiny rockets attached to the truck but at least the video did not appear before the trial began and it is difficult to assess what impact it may have had on the jury decision.

But more valid examples of litigation journalism are numerous. In Freehold, N.J., in 1988, parents sued a hospital for negligence, claiming their child suffered brain damage during surgery. Shortly after the suit was filed, a photo of the child undergoing therapy appeared on the front page of the regional newspaper along with details of the suit. The story was picked up by a New York City TV station, whose coverage included interviews with the parents.

Parents of a murdered student sued her university in 1988 and went on national talk shows to claim negligence. Several newspapers covered the story, even publishing photographs of the dead woman's room. The suit was settled out of court.

Most recently, a Florida widower, claiming his wife died from a brain tumor caused by her cellular telephone, argued his case on CNN's "Larry King Live."

Never mind that cellular phone company stock dropped the next day, and that the industry's reputation and solvency might have been damaged. Never mind that a layman was afforded credibility on an issue on which he was unqualified. Never mind that the public may have been needlessly alarmed. Never mind the merits of either side's case.

What we should mind is that litigation journalism is seriously undermining the integrity of our legal process.

First, the role of the courts is being pre-empted and their procedures undermined as more cases are tried in the public arena long before official hearings take place. The arguments are mostly one-sided, devoid of cross-examination, evidence or witnesses.

Second, while in the court of law a defendant can take the Fifth Amendment or decline to testify without prejudicing the case, in the court of the mass media, the defendant is expected to respond to questions and allegations. Failure to respond—resorting to "no comment"—is viewed as an admission of guilt.

This leads to a third point. Defendants in civil litigation are at a disadvantage when making pre-trial comments to the press. Anything they say can and will be used against them. How, without appearing callous, can a company argue in the court of public opinion that a plaintiff's child died because he misused the product, not because the product was defective?

Those who use the First Amendment to defend litigation journalism should remember the ethical requirements of fairness, balance and responsible reporting. Calling the defendants for a statement is not enough to insure fairness, nor is that a relevant point. Legal arguments are intended to be made before impartial judges and juries. It is not the function of the press, or of those who disseminate news and information on the fringes of journalism—like talk shows—to allow the merits of individual cases to be argued or promoted outside due process.

Those who cite the "people's right to know" argument should consider that the people have a right to know the truth. In litigation journalism, the facts are often never presented.

More often than not, the plaintiffs' basic motive for using the mass media is not to insure justice or aid public understanding but to secure financial reward. Many cases involving litigation journalism are about forcing out-of-court settlements and upping the ante in return for squashing the adverse publicity.

Even more insidious is the chilling effect such cases have. The mere threat of a suit, no matter how frivolous, is enough to force organizations or individuals to reach for their pocketbooks in return for the would-be plaintiff's silence.

Once again, due process is the loser.

What can be done? Certainly the press should not and cannot be prohibited from reporting when civil suits are filed and what the basic accusations are. And it must pursue its responsibility to report on issues where public health and safety might be involved. But this is quite different from letting plaintiffs have unchallenged air time and newspaper space to personalize their cases.

Bar associations should require members to follow the rules of evidence set by law, not the press. Public relations consultants should be held accountable by their professional associations for participating in litigation journalism. The practice counters the groups' codes of ethical standards requiring consultants to avoid corrupting the channels of communication and processes of government.

Finally, the media should review their ethical guidelines and consider whether short-term pocketbook interests are worth the long-term consequences to society.[12]

Carole Gorney's article is a clear and concise portrayal of the ills of litigation journalism.

For another approach, consider the following editorial, which also appeared in the *New York Times*:[13]

SHORT OF CASH, LONG ON PERSPECTIVE
Universities go back to the drawing board
by Michael I. Sovern

Despite the laments of purist critics and doomsday scenarists, the glory days of higher education are not all in the past. Yes, universities are cutting back, reducing faculties and services, putting building projects on hold. If money is scarce, critics are not. Forced by the recession, government cutbacks and higher costs (especially health benefits) to spend more and more time on fund-raising, university presidents are achieving successes in development campaigns, only to be assailed for spending too much time on fund-raising. When the prospect of less financial aid to students is raised, it is not the "education President" but the college president who comes under fire. Yet

[12]Carole Gorney, "Litigation Journalism is a Scourge;" *New York Times*, Feb. 15, 1993.

[13]*New York Times*, Feb. 15, 1993.

as Washington's support for students has waned, colleges have increased their contributions enormously.

Despite such ironies, I continue to view the 1990s as a particularly exciting time for the American university.

Before World War II, one out of every 10 young Americans sought a college degree. Today, fully one half of high school graduates will go on to college, a marvelous achievement even when we allow for the wide range in quality awaiting them. Today, students and their successors may benefit from the streamlining of universities that will result from the current financial squeeze.

Like many big institutions, our universities have grown rapidly with an exuberant belief that "more is better" and with too little attention to individual strengths and weaknesses. Thoughtful planning is now the order of the day. A likely outcome is a renaissance of the primary mission of the university, teaching. One of many heartening signs is the endowment of new named professorships at a number of institutions, including my own, to honor and support faculty excellence in the classroom. And because students and their families pay most of the faculty's salaries at independent colleges, tough economic times bring pressures on faculty to do more teaching.

Many colleges that traded rigorous learning for popularity during the upheavals of the 1960s have been returning to the core curriculum idea that originated at Columbia in 1919. At the same time, horizons have been expanding to add whole civilizations and an entire gender long slighted by conventional curriculums.

The government-university research partnership is not what it once was, and that is cause for serious concern. But even Japanese leaders, critical of many aspects of American life, continue to acknowledge that the American research university is the best in the world. Our leaders know this too. The growing challenge posed by international competition should lead to a strengthening of Federal support for American university-based research enterprise.

Even as universities like mine are picking up 90 percent of the student aid tab, they willingly take on other social responsibilities. This spring, a new Center on Addiction and Substance Abuse directed by Joseph A. Califano, Jr., the former Secretary of Health, Education and Welfare, was established at Columbia to bring together all professional disciplines in an effort to combat a plague that finds government, for all its activity, almost a helpless bystander.

The opportunities for universities to teach students about values through example are legion—by helping to strengthen local schools, standing fast in support of freedom of expression and treating all with whom we deal fairly and humanely.

Almost alone among contemporary institutions, we take the long view. The crisis of the moment must be managed, but we measure our success over generations. We are struggling to preserve our endowments precisely because our vision of service encompasses not just today's students but tomorrow's as well. In an era characterized by the evanescent—the quick buck and the empty political promise—the hallmark of America's universities remains the enduring.[14]

As the president of Columbia University, the author, Michael I. Sovern, presents a logical, thorough defense of the ways his institution is adapting to contemporary economic and social realities.

Two editorials, two different approaches—but several common elements. Both writers address an issue of current interest and controversy. Both focus on a central stand and back up claims with a variety of insights. Both editorials are uncomplicated and easy to read. A good editorial leaves a reader more knowledgeable and understanding about a particular issue.

Chapter Recap

In summary, responsive writing presents a company or client's point of view about a journalist's or newspaper's point of view; about a crisis; or about an issue.

Letters to the Editor

Letters to the editor can bring a client or point of view positive recognition. Do *not*, however, respond to a critical article that is accurate. Your response may bring new attention to the negative publicity.

Letters correcting mistakes and inaccuracies should include the following:

[14]Michael I. Sovern, "Short of Cash, Long on Perspective," *New York Times*, June 13, 1992.

- The date and page on which the incorrect article appeared
- The incorrect information that was printed
- The correct information that should have been stated
- The name and title of the author of the letter

In letters criticizing a reporter's conclusions, you should adhere to these guidelines:

- Support your points of contention with facts. Do not use emotional responses to defend your position.
- Keep your letter brief.
- Try not to bring in lawyers or threaten to pull advertising from the publication.
- Make your opinion clear and easily understood.
- State your case professionally and *tactfully*. There is no need for the tone of your letter to be accusatory, derogatory, or in any other way inflammatory.
- Maintain good relations with the media. Don't anger or alienate reporters with vitriolic and overly critical letters.

Letters serve as publicity tools by explaining why a company, product, client, or point of view should not have been left out of the article.

Official Statements

An official statement and possibly a background Q&A are prepared and approved so that company spokespersons can use them in interviews, news releases can follow their guidelines, and company editorials or letters to the editor can present the official company point of view.

Crisis Releases

Develop a companywide crisis response plan that has the advance approval of senior management and legal counsel and that includes the following:

- An assessment of the company's vulnerabilities
- Company background information to be provided to the press

- Provision for a crisis information and rumor control center, interview areas, and information management teams
- Prepared, fill-in-the blanks news releases for the media, the public, and the employees
- Home phone numbers for all key people, plus a companywide phone list
- Provisions for media access and escorts on company property

In preparing crisis releases, follow these guidelines:

- Gauge the scope of interest your crisis is likely to attract.
- Use bullets in writing the facts.
- Release all information on official letterhead.
- Put a date and time on top of every page.
- Include the name and telephone number of a person who can be contacted twenty-four hours a day.
- Double- or triple-space the information in the release.
- Consult with legal counsel before releasing information.

To minimize negative reports, take these steps:

- Provide television news staff members with videotape and/or live reports from the scene, as well as interview opportunities to bring a story to life, so they will *not* continue to rerun shots of the disaster.
- Prepare press kits that include background information a reporter can use to put the current incident into context.
- Keep a log of what information was released, when, and to whom.
- Consider the use of answering-machine messages and a priority answering system to handle phone inquiries.
- Design a standard procedure for quick responses, news conferences, and regularly scheduled briefings (see Chapter 6 for information about arranging special events).

Guest Editorials

To be selected from the numerous submissions to publications, op-ed pieces should be brief and be timely, present a strong point of view, and have a prestigious byline.

10

Program Writing

Selling Your Concept to the Client

A program is the blueprint for public relations campaigns. It is what a client buys from a public relations agency, or what an in-house department often submits for budget approval within an organization. The program maps out the goals and strategies of a public relations campaign.

One of the more famous public relations programs was devised by Edward L. Bernays, the "founding father" of public relations. Bernays was asked by the makers of Ivory soap to invent a way to change the negative attitude children had toward soap. His solution? Ivory sponsored a soap-carving contest that ultimately had 22 million kids across America submitting soap sculptures.

Writing a public relations campaign is a challenging and important task. Programs are often written under tight deadlines, yet require careful analysis and creative thinking. The secret to writing a good public relations program is to have a solid understanding of a client's needs and goals, coupled with innovative ideas that are put forth in brief, incisive writing.

The Structure of a Public Relations Program

Written programs can take many forms, depending primarily on the style and format preferred by the organization or individuals who approve them. Some corporations insist that a program be no longer than two typewritten pages. Others prefer a program set forth in large binders containing detailed market research and other supporting data. In this chapter, we will review a basic formula for creating a public relations program that can be tailored to different organizational writing requirements.

This formula comprises the following categories, each of which will be discussed in detail:

- Introduction/situation analysis
- Objectives
- Target audiences
- Strategies
- Activities
- Management, staffing, and administration
- Budget

Let's assume you have been asked to devise a program to support the sales of a new brand of Mayflower blue jeans called "30" jeans. Following is a step-by-step primer for developing your public relations program.

Introduction/Situation Analysis

The opening section of the program describes the reason the program is being written and raises all the issues the program is designed to answer. This section is usually called the introduction, or—because it summarizes the situation necessitating a public relations program—the situation analysis.

Mayflower Jeans has come to you because it is introducing a new model of blue jeans into the market. The distinguishing feature of these jeans is their prewashed look, and they are targeted to the fourteen- to twenty-one-year-old market. The Mayflower people have supplied you with ample background—they have told you the principal competitors, the current sales trends for denim, the results of their test marketing, the theme of their advertising campaign, and so on. What you must do now is to go one step further and dig up even more information that will help you develop the ideas you need for your program. Find out in which media outlets your client wants or deserves coverage. Research the interests and buying habits of fourteen- to twenty-one-year-olds. Look up information in programs being used by competitors.

The introduction section of your program should summarize the data you've collected and describe the challenge facing "30" blue jeans. Generally, introductions should not exceed one to three double-spaced pages in length. Yours might begin like this:

INTRODUCTION

Blue jeans are no longer the first choice in casual fashion. As new styles, such as the "sweatsuit" look and the "sixties" look, emerge, the traditional all-American denim look is losing popularity. Shipments of denim were down 34 percent for the first six months of this year, and the trend seems to be continuing.

Mayflower Jeans must re-create excitement in blue jeans and capture the attention of the teenage market with its new model "30" jeans. Research shows that today's teenagers like to consider themselves rebellious, but are nevertheless attracted to traditional values, such as upward mobility, stability, and fitness.

This public relations program is designed to capitalize on the sexy and rebellious image of "30" jeans, yet cater to the traditional desires of today's teens. The program is intended to build awareness of and excitement for "30" jeans by drawing widespread attention to the product through a series of teen-geared activities that will generate mass-media coverage.

The goals for the introduction are to demonstrate your knowledge and understanding of the client's needs and to build excitement and interest in the program that follows. When you write an introduction, make sure you answer the following questions:

- Have you adequately explained the public relations challenge facing the client?
- Have you demonstrated your understanding of the situation with solid facts and figures?
- Is the introduction written in such a way that it compels the reader to review the program?
- Is it three pages or shorter?

If the answer to all these questions is yes, then it is time to move on to the objectives section of the program.

Objectives

The objectives of the program should be listed with bullets rather than written in paragraph form. The objectives for your program might be written as follows:

OBJECTIVES

The public relations program for "30" jeans is designed to do the following:

- Create excitement about and national awareness of "30" jeans
- Increase sales of "30" jeans
- Establish "30" jeans as the jeans of choice for teenagers

The objectives are stated clearly and concisely; there is no need to add flowery prose, and you should never obscure the meaning of the sentences. Like all the other parts of a public relations program, the objectives should be straightforward and demonstrate your understanding of the client's needs.

Once you have established your objectives, you then present the target audiences.

Target Audiences

The target audiences section of the program helps you as well as the client. As you research the target audiences and decide whom your program is trying to reach, you will begin to focus your thoughts on what type of people the program is aimed at. The target audiences section helps define your activities, strategies, and objectives.

When writing the target audiences section, list the various audiences in bullet form. There is no need to write this section in paragraph form; it will be self-explanatory. The target audiences section of your program could be written like this:

TARGET AUDIENCES

- MALES AND FEMALES AGES FOURTEEN TO TWENTY-ONE
  Middle- to high-income families
  Fashion-minded teens
  Leaders of peer groups

- PARENTS OF TEENAGERS
- OPINION LEADERS FOR TEENS
  Teachers
  Professional athletes
  TV/movie personalities
  Rock stars
- CLOTHING RETAILERS
- MEDIA
  Fashion writers
  Entertainment editors
  Society-page editors

Note that the categories that require elaboration (such as opinion leaders) are broken down into specific subgroups. The target audiences section serves as a guideline for the program's activities. After developing your activities, check them against the target audiences list to make sure they coordinate with and complement one another.

Strategies

You have now set the stage for the program, outlined its objectives, and established whom it will reach. The next step is to describe your strategies. The strategies section should outline the methods or vehicles you will use to achieve your objectives and reach your target audiences.

This section describes, in broad terms, the channels you will be using to communicate your messages. If your program calls for one-on-one interviews with security analysts, that would be mentioned in the strategies section. If the program is built on word-of-mouth publicity for a product, that would also be described in this section.

As with the objectives and target audiences sections, the strategies section should be in bulleted form and its points stated briefly. The strategies section for your "30" jeans program might look like this:

STRATEGIES

To accomplish program objectives, we have developed the following strategies:

- Generate enthusiasm for "30" jeans by associating them with well-known teenage celebrities.
- Create excitement over "30" jeans through a national contest for teenagers.
- Work with retailers to establish "30" jeans special events that will bring more teenagers into their stores.
- Establish visibility for "30" jeans by having them worn in motion pictures.
- Make "30" jeans a "must have" article of clothing for the target audiences.

The strategies should describe—again, in broad terms—how you will achieve your objectives. This is quite different from the activities section, which describes in detail the actual work you'll be performing for the client.

Activities

The activities section of the program requires the most creative thought and is the most important part of any program. It is here that you unveil your specific ideas for promoting "30" jeans. It is here that Edward L. Bernays would describe his concept of a national soap-carving contest for kids.

Each of the previous sections has been building toward the activities section. The ideas in the activities section are what a client will be scrutinizing closely.

When developing the activities section, describe individual activities in paragraph form, keeping in mind these guidelines:

- Demonstrate how the activity is suited to the target audiences for your program.
- Explain why the activity is likely to get media attention.
- Establish why the idea is suited to your client or product. (In other words, *how* will this idea sell more blue jeans?)
- Cover all your bases. Do not leave any glaring unanswered questions. Anticipate all of the possible questions the client might ask about logistics, markets, and other concerns.
- Keep it brief. Get right to the point with your idea and explain why it will work.

The activities section of your "30" jeans program might look like this:

A. JAMES DEAN LOOK-ALIKE CONTEST

The James Dean look of the mid-1950s is popular again among teenagers. Dean represents rebellious youth, yet his 1950s status makes him nostalgic and all-American for today's young people. We recommend that "30" jeans sponsor a national James Dean look-alike contest.

All entrants would be required to wear "30" jeans during the contest. Entry forms would be picked up in the "30" jeans section at retail stores. The grand-prize winner would win thirty hundred-dollar bills, and would become the "30" jeans man in your "30" jeans advertising campaign.

There would be five regional winners, each of whom would be publicized in his local market, and the national finals would be held in Hollywood.

B. "30" JEANS NIGHT AT THE BALLPARK

To create a "must have" excitement about "30" jeans, we recommend that Mayflower Jeans work with stadiums in selected target markets to sponsor a "30" jeans night at the ballpark, during which everyone wearing "30" jeans gets into the ballpark at half price. This will generate visibility for the jeans, and will add incentive for kids to purchase the jeans. We will work to publicize the events in local newspapers to gain more awareness for "30" jeans.

Your own goal in writing the activities section is to create enthusiasm for your ideas. You must sell the client on the concept and demonstrate how and why it will work. Above all, you must explain how the specific ideas will help sell more of the client's product.

While every program is designed differently for each client, and there is no set number of activities a program should contain, the number of activities is usually governed by the size of the budget—the bigger the budget, the more flexibility you have in your activities.

Management, Staffing, and Administration

Now that you have laid out the creative portion of the program, it's time to explain who will implement the campaign and how much it will cost. If you're submitting the program as an independent consultant or on behalf of a public relations agency, you'll need to include a section on management, staffing, and administration. This section typically answers the following questions:

Management. Who from your agency will oversee the program? Why is he or she particularly well suited to the task? What relevant experience does this manager have?

Staffing. Who is responsible for day-to-day implementation? How many staffers will work on this account? What are their roles? Why are they qualified for those roles?

Administration. Who are the primary contacts for the client? What is the timetable for implementing the program? What subcontractors or consultants will be used?

Remember that in this section of the program, you are trying to convince your client or management that you have a competent team and adequate resources to meet the stated objectives. Typically, this section will include brief biographies of the account team that will be implementing the program. (For guidance on how to structure a biography, see Chapter 3.)

Budget

After laying out the mechanics of how your program can be implemented, you must now explain the true bottom line—the budget.

Budgets can be presented in many formats, but one practical method is simply to attach a cost to each of the activities you are proposing in your program. This allows your client or management to take a "menu" approach to selecting activities when budgets are limited.

If you are submitting a program on behalf of a public relations agency, you must also include a budget for the staff time your agency will expend on the client's behalf. Agencies and consultants typically bill their time based on an hourly rate.

One way to lay out the budget is to provide a quick summary of costs that includes a line item for each activity. Attached to the summary would be a more detailed look at how you arrived at your cost estimates. Thus, the summary of your budget for the "30" jeans program might look like this:

ACTIVITY	COST
A. Look-alike contest	$265,000
B. Night at the ballpark	$260,000
TOTAL PROGRAM COST:	$525,000

For the detailed estimate, it is helpful to provide as accurate a breakdown as possible of the costs involved in the activities. A detailed estimate of activity A, for example, might look like this:

A. James Dean look-alike contest	Cost
Collateral materials (Entry forms, point-of-purchase displays, posters for 1,000 retail outlets)	$ 30,000
Press kits (Photographs, news releases, fact sheets, backgrounders; 2,000 kits)	$ 10,000
Prizes (10,000 key chains, 5 regional cash awards, 1 grand prize)	$ 45,000
Press conferences (5 regional conferences and 1 national conference; facility, catering, AV)	$ 60,000
Travel and entertainment (Media lunches, agency travel, general expenses)	$ 16,000
Agency fee Vice-president 120 hours at $200/hour Account supervisor 200 hours at $150/hour Account executive 250 hours at $100/hour Account executive 250 hours at $100/hour	$104,000
TOTAL	$265,000

Similarly, you would next lay out a detailed breakdown of costs for implementing the night-at-the-ballpark activity.

Be aware that the budget items do *not* reflect the actual amount per hour paid by the agency to the public relations executive or the actual cost of each activity to the agency. Each item here includes the agency markup according to formulas the agency has established to cover overhead, benefits, expenses, new business development, and, it is hoped, a profit.

The level of detail in your budget will vary according to client or organizational demand, but suffice it to say that you should not submit a price estimate without thoroughly researching the true cost of implementing a program. Your company's profit and ultimately your job will depend on the viability of your budget and your ability to manage your projects so that you bring your activities in on budget.

Chapter Recap

In summary, public relations programs can take many written forms, but all should be written with the needs of the client in mind. Some people prefer one- or two-page documents with bulleted points, while others want to see reams of data. Regardless of the format, all should strive to include the following salient information:

- An introduction/situation analysis
- Clearly stated objectives
- An explanation of the target audiences
- Strategies to achieve your objectives
- Activities that follow the strategies
- An outline of the management, staffing, and administration needed for implementation
- A realistic and detailed budget or cost estimate

Appendix A

Research and Interview Techniques

Research is the key to all informed and effective writing. As applied to public relations writing, research is essentially a fact-finding process that enables you to evaluate information in terms of ideas and distinctions.

Books, magazines, and newspapers are the primary sources for research. Interviewing knowledgeable sources is also a vital component of researching, but it is usually better to seek out published information before interviewing a source.

You should begin your research by obtaining as much existing written material on your subject as you can. Visit your local library; if you work in a public relations office, check the files related to your subject and call any place that might supply relevant literature.

If your company or agency subscribes to an electronic clipping or information service, you can, for example, search for printed newspaper and/or magazine articles by topic, company, or product, or by the name of a person, such as an interview subject or a journalist.

Talk with people in the field you are researching before you schedule any formal interviews. Collect background tidbits and impressions, and pay attention to the adjectives people use in describing your subject. You may discover information unavailable from published sources and gain hints that will prove valuable when you conduct interviews.

Decide if you want to tape-record the interview or write notes by hand. Some interviewers do both; because it is too time-consuming to type complete transcripts of taped interviews, they write from their notes and then use the tape to confirm the quotes and figures.

Make sure that your tape recorder is working, that you have

enough blank tapes, that the sound level is adequate for the distance between the person and the microphone, and that you set the recorder so that you can tell when the tape runs out. At the start of the interview, you might say, "I'd like to tape-record this, if you don't mind, so I can double-check quotes and figures."

Since you are interviewing for public relations writing, not journalism, you may or may not want to offer to let the person check the quotes. In any case, the people you are interviewing within the company or the client's company may be given approval over your writing. Since quotes and information given you by less senior staffers may be attributed to their boss or to the CEO in the final version of your piece, those lower in the hierarchy should probably be told who in their area will be giving final approval over what you write and that you are interviewing them for background information, not necessarily to quote them.

Because improvisation rarely works well, never go into an interview unprepared. You should be equipped with a list of specific questions that were not answered in the literature you read. Good research techniques keep you from wasting time on commonplace information during the interview and allow you to use the time in an efficient, enlightening, and engaging manner. Of course, there may be times when you want to confirm a documented fact or two, but let the subject know that you are doing just that, and move through it quickly. Nothing disenchants an interviewee faster than an interviewer who has not done his or her homework. Conversely, an effective way to keep your subject's interest and involvement is to show, through intelligent, informed questions, that you know to whom you are talking and what you are talking about.

Listen carefully during the interview. Don't be so fixed on your prepared questions that you can't respond naturally to what is being said or pick up on an interesting angle you hadn't anticipated. Establishing a rapport with your interviewee will yield better, more complete, and more honest responses.

Ask qualitative questions. You are seeking the most illuminating, descriptive answers possible. Rarely do you want a simple yes or no response. For example, if you are interviewing a novice diver who accompanied Jacques Cousteau on a scuba expedition, you do *not* want to ask, "Did you have difficulties as a novice diver?" Rather, ask, "*What* were your difficulties as a novice diver?" It's a subtle difference, but one that will help elicit the kinds of responses you can better use to let quotations tell the story.

Finally, when interviewing, never hesitate to ask your subject to explain something if you are not 100 percent certain about what he or she is saying. Ask about a word or reference if you are unsure about it. Always ask, "What do you mean by that?" or "Do you mean . . . ?" and summarize what you think the interviewee is saying. There is no such thing as a dumb question. It's dumb not to ask. Those who are afraid to ask will never know. Sure, you should be pretty well informed from all the research you've done, but communication is a delicate process, and you should, as much as possible, confirm that you understand what is being said.

In summary, doing research, including interviewing, before you start to write is key to effective writing. Your sources may include these:

- Books
- Magazines
- Newspapers
- Electronic data bases
- Material on file
- People in the field
- Interviews

When interviewing someone, follow these guidelines:

- Research thoroughly.
- Prepare specific questions that are not already answered by your research.
- Tape-record the interview and/or write out notes.
- Listen carefully.
- Ask qualitative questions.
- Ask follow-up questions.
- If you don't understand something, ask.

Appendix B

Creating and Maintaining Press Lists

A press list, also called a media list, is exactly what it sounds like: a list of targeted press outlets that is used for distributing information to the press.

The press list is one of the most fundamental tools of any media-oriented public relations campaign. If the list is inaccurate or incomplete, the campaign will suffer accordingly.

Press lists are compiled from directories, newsletters, personal contacts, and other sources. It is important to learn how to compile, maintain, and use a press list by examining the various resource materials available (these will be discussed later in this appendix). There are specific methods for organizing the press list efficiently and then putting it to good use.

Creating and maintaining a press list are hardly glamorous tasks, but they are jobs of vital importance. Compiling a press list is akin to graduating from public relations basic training: It is time-consuming and can be tedious, but everyone must do it at some point in a public relations career.

Most clients retain public relations professionals because of their expertise in understanding and dealing with the press.

A good example of the importance of an accurate press list involves one of the top five public relations agencies in the United States. The agency had submitted a press list as part of the final-selection round of a competitive pitch to win an account with one of America's largest banks. The agency lost the account, however, when the bank discovered that two of the most important publications in its industry, the *ABA Banking Journal* and *American*

Banker, were not included in the agency's press list. It was merely an oversight, but a costly one.

In addition to losing credibility with clients or management, a faulty press list angers another key audience: the press. Mark Goldstein, an editor for *Industry Week* magazine, estimates that 80 percent of the press material he receives in the mail goes straight into the trash because it is not applicable to what he covers. This problem exists, he says, because his name is thoughtlessly included on all kinds of press lists for announcements that very often are of no interest to him. The key to avoiding serious errors and omissions lies in careful research and attention to details.

Examining Resources and Materials

There are many useful reference books that list the names, addresses, and editorial scopes of magazines, newspapers, and radio and television stations and programs.

Here are the most commonly used directories:

- *Ayer's Directory of Newspapers and Magazines*
  N. W. Ayers & Sons
  210 West Washington Square
  Philadelphia, PA 19106
- *Bacon's Publicity Checker*
  R. H. Bacon Publishing Company
  332 Michigan Avenue
  Chicago, IL 60604
- *Editor & Publisher's Yearbook*
  Editor & Publisher Company
  850 Third Avenue
  New York, NY 10022
- *National Radio Publicity Directory*
  Peter Glenn Publications
  17 East Forty-eighth Street
  New York, NY 10017
- *New York Publicity Outlets*
  TV Publicity Outlets
  Public Relations Plus, Inc.

Box 327
Washington Depot, CT 06794
* *Radio Contacts*
  Television Contacts
  Cable Contacts
  TV News Contacts
  Syndicated Columnist Contacts
  News Bureau Contacts
  BPI Media Services
  P.O. Box 2015
  Lakewood NY 08701
* *Standard Rate and Data Service*
  Standard Rate and Data Services, Inc.
  5021 Old Orchard Road
  Skokie, IL 60076

The above-listed publications are updated regularly and contain detailed descriptions of publications, including editors' names, addresses, and phone numbers, as well as descriptions of editorial content.

Devising Categories

Once the source materials have been gathered, the next step in creating a press list is to outline the categories the list should encompass. Every list must be tailored to the needs of a specific client. For example, a press list for sex therapist Dr. Ruth Westheimer's public relations campaign will be entirely different from a list for a General Motors campaign. There is no such thing as a generic press list that can be used for any client.

In creating press list categories, it is necessary to understand a client's public relations objectives. The categories must cover all areas that might serve as likely outlets for news about your client. In general, a press list will consist of the following categories:

* Wire services
* Daily newspapers
* News and general interest publications
* Business publications

- Men's and women's interest magazines
- Primary industry trade publications
- Vertical industry trade publications
- News syndicates and syndicated columnists
- Television and cable
- Radio
- Special-interest mailings

Let's review each of the categories and examine their structure, function, and importance in a press list.

Wire Services

The wire service category would include the Associated Press, United Press International, Reuters, Ltd., and Dow Jones News Service. Wire services supply news to various media on a subscription basis. For a set fee, wire services supply newspapers, magazines, and radio and TV stations with stories reported from all over the world. The wire services are extremely vital resources, because they reach thousands of media outlets.

Wire services are set up like newspapers, in that they have editors assigned to specific beats, or subjects. For example, Associated Press has a science editor, an automotive editor, a TV editor, and so on. In addition, the wire services have local bureaus throughout the world to cover breaking news. Thus, if a client is opening a multimillion-dollar factory in Wentzville, it would make sense to contact the Associated Press bureau in nearby St. Louis to alert it to the event.

In addition to specific industry editors, the wire services have full news staffs to cover breaking news. Except for feature editors, most wire service reporters work on extremely tight deadlines and need to be informed of breaking news as quickly as possible.

When compiling the wire service category of a press list, you must examine the target audience for the client. If the news announcements for which the list is being used are computer-oriented, then the wire service category should contain the name of the computer, information processing, or high-technology editor. If the announcements are finance-oriented, the list should contain the names of financial editors. Tailor the listings to the subject of the news announcement.

It is important to know which bureau of the wire service handles the type of news being announced. For instance, a government-related announcement will probably be handled by the Washington bureau of a wire service, and a show-business announcement will probably be handled by the Los Angeles bureau. Determining the correct bureau can be as simple as calling the wire service and asking.

Daily Newspapers

The daily newspaper is a staple of most people's reading diets. The importance of a daily newspaper in a public relations campaign depends, of course, on the needs of a client.

In compiling the newspaper category, you must determine which cities should be included in the press list, and whether local angles will appear in the client's upcoming news announcements. A story about a new type of snow plow, for example, will not be of much interest to the *Miami Herald* or the *Tucson Star*.

Most daily newspapers require a local news angle in their stories. Aside from the largest newspapers, such as the *New York Times,* the *Los Angeles Times,* the *Washington Post,* the *Wall Street Journal, USA Today,* and a handful of others, most dailies rely on the wire services and news syndicates to supply their national and worldwide news. Thus, daily newspapers are mostly included in special press lists that are compiled for targeted regional media events or announcements. If an event is being conducted in Denver, Salt Lake City, and Phoenix, then a press list must be compiled that includes the daily newspapers in each of those cities and their surrounding areas. Since large cities often have numerous local papers, weeklies, and neighborhood newspapers, you also need to pay attention to each paper's circulation and area of distribution.

The editors who are most often included in press lists are those covering special sections, such as fashion, life-styles, science, and business. The source materials listed earlier, such as *Bacon's Publicity Checker,* list the names of the editors covering each of these special sections. *Bacon's* breaks down special sections into twenty-two categories:

1. Automotive
2. Book review

3. Business and financial
4. Editorial page
5. Education
6. Environment and ecology
7. Farm
8. Fashion
9. Food
10. Home furnishings
11. Radio and television
12. Real estate
13. Science
14. Sports
15. Travel
16. Women's
17. Entertainment
18. Medical and health
19. Outdoor
20. Life-style
21. Garden
22. Computers

When deciding which sections of which newspapers to include in a press list, the most important criteria are the type of news announcements and the geographic markets that have applicable local story angles. Ask yourself these questions to determine whether a particular daily newspaper should be on your press list:

- Does the announcement you're making concern an event taking place in or around the city this paper is based in?
- Does the announcement mention any people who are from that city?
- Is the product or service you're announcing available in that city?
- Does your client have a substantial presence in that city?
- If you lived in that city, would you be interested in the announcement?

If you answered no to all of the above questions, you should not include that particular paper on your list.

News and General Interest Publications

News and general interest publications include *Newsweek, Time, U.S. News & World Report,* and *Life.* These are national publications with very large circulations, and they generally require stories that are of national or international scope.

The news weeklies like *Time* concentrate most heavily on "hard" news events, such as wars, disasters, elections, and political developments. There has been a recent trend, however, toward increasing coverage of such subjects as business, life-style, art, television, movies, and other areas that offer opportunities for public relations placements.

In addition, a number of publications—such as *People, US,* and *Life*—offer human interest stories.

Business Publications

Articles that appear in business publications like *Fortune, Forbes, Business Week,* and the *Wall Street Journal* can result in very prestigious and influential exposure for a company and are usually mandatory elements of any business-oriented press list.

The major business publications require stories that are of national interest. In most cases, these publications have editors assigned to specific industries—computers, automobiles, steel, electronics, agriculture, and so forth. Many editors even cover specific companies as part of their beat.

Most business magazines contain a section on breaking news or new developments but consist mainly of feature stories on individual companies or industry trends. In assembling the business publication section of a press list, it is again crucial to know which editor covers a client's industry.

In addition to national publications, there are a growing number of local business journals, such as *Crain's Chicago Business* or the *St. Louis Business Journal,* which, of course, require local angles.

Men's and Women's Interest Publications

Men's interest publications include *GQ* and *Playboy;* women's interest publications include *McCall's* and *Ladies' Home Journal.*

These are national publications that cover topics of specific interest to men or women. Each publication has regular departments and columns that offer good opportunities for a public relations campaign.

The best way to decide which publications—and which editors at these publications—should be included in a press list is to read through each of the magazines and note which columns and departments are suitable for a particular client.

Primary Industry Trade Publications

There are trade publications covering everything from electronic toys to hog chow, and many of them are extremely important to their respective industries. Primary trades are those which focus directly on your client's industry.

Often the best way to determine which industry trade publications are the most important for your client is to ask executives who know the industry well. It is extremely important to research the area of trade publications, because it is easy to list inappropriate publications. For example, big differences exist between the coverage in *Electronic News,* which provides general information on industry trends and development, and that in *Electronics Week,* which provides more in-depth technical coverage of products and technology. When compiling a list for an electronics company, you must be aware of these differences.

Industry trade publications are highly specific in their coverage, and it is crucial to include the name of the correct editor on a press list. For example, *Electronic News* has different editors for semiconductors, consumer electronics, military electronics, components, distribution, and other specific topics. If a client makes consumer TV sets, then the press list should include the name of the consumer electronics editor, rather than the industrial components editor.

Vertical Industry Trade Publications

Most companies sell their products in a variety of markets. For example, a furniture manufacturer might sell products to offices, schools, hotels, and individual homeowners. In this case, offices, schools, hotels, and homeowners are called vertical markets.

When putting together a press list, you must include vertical market trade publications. Thus, for a furniture-manufacturing client whose primary trade publications include *Home Furnishings Daily, Furniture Production and Design,* and *Furniture Manufacturing Management,* a comprehensive press list would also include vertical trade publications, such as *Today's Office, School Product News,* and *Hotel and Motel Management.*

News Syndicates and Syndicated Columnists

In addition to the wire services that offer national and international distribution, there are a great many news syndicates. Offering extensive reach from a central source, these organizations include Copley News Services, the Fairchild Syndicate, Gannett News Service, and the Newspaper Enterprise Association. Also available are special interest news services, such as the Black Press Service, the Hispanic Link Service, the Jewish Telegraphic Agency, Science News, and the College News Bureau.

Many news services, such as the Los Angeles Times Syndicate, are divisions of newspapers and operate like the Associated Press and other wire services, in that they are set up to offer smaller papers with limited staff resources the option to buy stories for publication. Others, such as Gannett News Services or the Fairchild Syndicate, are set up to service only publications within a particular publishing group, such as Gannett Newspapers or Fairchild Publications.

The best way to find the news services and syndicates that are most appropriate for a particular press list is simply to call up and find out what type of service is offered.

Another valuable outlet for publicity is the syndicated columnist. Well-known syndicated columnists include Mike Royko, Sylvia Porter, Dan Dorfman, and Joey Sasso. Most syndicated columnists have an area of specialization. For example, Sasso covers the entertainment industry, Dorfman covers Wall Street, and Porter offers money-making tips.

For researching syndicated columnists, use *Syndicated Columnist Contacts,* published by BPI Media Services (see the list of directories above). Most syndicated columnists can be contacted directly and welcome public relations materials.

Television and Cable

Perhaps the best way to communicate a message to millions of people instantly is through a network-television show. An appearance on a morning network-news show like "Good Morning America" or "Today" will be seen by well over 5 million viewers.

In addition to news shows, magazine-format programs, which are gaining in popularity, have opened up many new potential placements for public relations campaigns. "Sixty Minutes," "Entertainment Tonight," and "E! Television" all use the magazine format.

Because of the rapid rate of show cancellations and personnel turnover in the TV industry, most television press lists become quickly outdated. It is necessary to update a TV press list frequently by calling the show, station, or network; never trust a television press list to be current and accurate.

For a client, television offers valuable exposure both locally and nationally. Most television sections of press lists are tailored to individual projects, such as media tours, new product introductions, or concert or performance tours. In addition to local news programs, countless talk shows and guest-oriented programs exist in local markets, and the expansion of cable programming has introduced many new shows and formats.

Most talk shows and interview programs have talent coordinators, who select guests and work with producers to put shows together. In most cases, the talent coordinator's name should be on a press list. Television, however, is a highly collaborative medium, and people other than talent coordinators may make, or help make, decisions on booking guests. They may have titles such as associate producer, researcher, or talent booker.

News shows have assignment editors, who select what should be covered in a given news segment. Because TV news has such limited time in producing a show, these editors seldom commit ahead of time to covering events like press conferences. Television reporters can show up only at the last minute, provided that other, breaking news doesn't compete with yours. It is the assignment editor who should be on your press list for TV news shows.

As mentioned earlier, most television sections of press lists are tailored to individual projects. Television publicity is most often sought for either publicity tours or special events. If a client is conducting a publicity tour in Chicago, St. Louis, and Denver, for example, it would be necessary to compile a press list that includes all possible television appearances in these three cities. Aside from the news programs in each of these cities, the list would contain such shows as "Denver Showcase," "A.M. Chicago," "Today in Chicago," and "Eve on St. Louis."

Radio

The radio section of a press list is similar to the television section, in that it is usually tailored to a special event or publicity tour and needs constant updating. A major difference in producing radio press lists, however, is the number of national networks and syndicated shows.

Unlike television, which offers only three major broadcast networks, radio offers more than fifteen networks, each of which contains anywhere from 75 to 2,000 affiliated stations across the country. This means there are more opportunities for national exposure on radio than on television. Each of the radio networks offers a variety of programs that accept guests and have interview formats.

As with television, news programs at radio stations have assignment editors, and interview shows have talent coordinators. Local markets offer thousands of radio talk shows and interview possibilities.

Special Interest Mailings

In most every press list, you will have a special list of names that must be included for your mailings. These people may not be members of the press, but they should receive your information. They might include client personnel, industry members, important dealers or distributors of your client's product, your colleagues, and numerous other interested parties.

Compiling Entries

Once the categories have been identified for the overall press list, it is time to start compiling the entries. The best way to construct an entry is to list this information:

Name of editor
Title of editor
Name of publication
Address
Phone number

Phone numbers will not be printed on mailing labels, but it is useful to record them because press lists are also used for conducting follow-up calls to media personnel after the mailing has gone out.

Thus, a typical listing might read as follows:

Mr. Paul Carrol
Technology Editor
Wall Street Journal
22 Cortlandt Street
New York, NY 10007
(212) 285–5000

or

Bob Groves
Assignment Editor
WNWS-AM News
8000 Southwest Sixty-seventh Avenue
Miami, FL 33143
(305) 665–4833

It is important to note the editor's beat, if possible, for quick identification in the future. For example, there are dozens of editors working at the *Wall Street Journal.* If a press list records only the editor's name, you will have to make a phone call every time a release goes out to determine what area that particular editor covers. Also, if that particular editor leaves or changes positions, your release may get lost in the shuffle. With both the name and the position in the address, your release has a better chance of getting to the new editor.

When first compiling the press list, you will have to call almost every publication to determine the name of the correct editor to record on the press list. In *Bacon's Publicity Checker,* for example, the only editor listed for *Newsweek* magazine is Richard M. Smith, editor-in-chief. The editor-in-chief, however, is probably not the most suitable person to receive press releases for a particular client. A phone call must be made to determine the correct editor's name. For example, if a client is in the entertainment industry, you must call *Newsweek* and ask who the entertainment editor is; if a client is in computers, you must ask who the computer editor is; and so on.

It is important to research each individual entry on a press list, and it is best to call a publication, even if the directory lists the areas of specialty assigned to individual editors. This double-checking is necessary because editors often switch to other publications or change reporting beats.

Maintaining and Updating the Press List

Keeping a press list accurate and updated is an ongoing task that requires constant attention. There are several resources for keeping a list updated. One such resource is the press itself. Most publications list the following information about their editors:

- Changes
- Promotions
- Deaths or resignations

Each time a publication lists an editorial change, that change should be made on your master press list. In addition, there are several newsletters, magazines, and services for the public relations and journalism fields—such as *PR Aides, Businesswire Newsletter,* and *Editor & Publisher*—that list personnel changes and location moves.

Organizing the List

Because a press list can contain hundreds, even thousands, of names and addresses, it is extremely important to organize the list in a way that makes it easy to use. There are many ways to organize a list, but perhaps the most effective is to arrange the list alphabetically by category. This means the list is divided into categories, and each category is alphabetized by *program or publication* names, not by editor names.

A sample category would be organized as follows:

CATEGORY: GENERAL BUSINESS

Howard Muson
Editor
Across the Board
845 Third Avenue
New York, NY 10022
(212) 759–0900

Richard A. Donnelly
Commodities Editor
Barron's National Business and Financial Weekly
22 Cortlandt Street
New York, NY 10007
(212) 285–5243

William Holstein
International Business Editor
Business Week
1221 Avenue of the Americas
New York, NY 10020
(212) 512–2000

Otis Port
Technology Editor
Business Week
1221 Avenue of the Americas
New York, NY 10020
(212) 512–2000

Roy Nishida
Foreign Editor
Economic World
60 East Forty-second Street
New York, NY 10017
(212) 986–1588

John Conway
Trends Editor
Forbes Magazine
60 Fifth Avenue

New York, NY 10011
(212) 620–2200

Kathleen Wiegener
Semiconductor Editor
Forbes Magazine
12233 West Olympic Boulevard
Los Angeles, CA 90064
(213) 555–1212

Each category would be listed in that manner, except in the radio and television sections, which might be best broken down geographically, or alphabetically by state.

Getting the News Out Quickly and Efficiently

Some news releases must be sent to reporters within a matter of minutes, some overnight, and some in a few days. Let's discuss the various ways to send out news releases, and which methods to use in what circumstances.

Here are the most common methods for sending out news releases:

- Mail
- Messenger
- Facsimile
- News wires
- Overnight mail
- Telephone
- Electronic mail

Mail

Using the U.S. Postal Service is perhaps the easiest and least expensive method of distributing a news announcement, particularly in the case of a mass mailing, but it is also the slowest method. For a breaking news story, the mail cannot be used to send releases to outlets that have hourly or daily deadlines. On the other hand, the mail can be used for getting releases to magazines that have lengthy lead times and are not under deadline pressure on breaking news.

When using the mail for distributing a press release, you should send out the releases a few days earlier than the dateline of the release. In other words, if a release is dated March 17, send the release through the mail on March 14, and note in bold characters that the release must be held (embargoed) until March 17. Sending the release out in advance avoids the embarrassment and futility of having an editor receive a March 17 story on March 21.

Messenger

Aside from hopping into a car and delivering a news release in person, the next best way to deliver photos, documents, or packages quickly to the local newspaper or radio or TV station is by using a messenger, or courier service.

When sending a reporter an important news release, you should call the editor first and alert him or her to the fact that a messenger is on the way with the news release. Be sure to find out the floor or apartment number of the recipient, and leave a phone number with the messenger in case any problems arise.

Facsimile

Facsimile machines transmit documents through telephone wires and offer an excellent method for sending announcements anywhere in the world in a matter of minutes. Thus, if a reporter in Los Angeles immediately needs a news release from a public relations office in New York, the facsimile machine can transmit the document within minutes, or even seconds.

The major drawbacks to using facsimile machines are that sending copies to many different outlets takes a lot of time, the facsimile machine in newsrooms may be busy for long periods at a time, and photographs cannot be sent with the release.

News Wires

There are two services, PR Newswire and Businesswire, that offer instant distribution of a news release into thousands of newsrooms across the country. These news wires are set up like the Associated Press and United Press International and have teletype terminals installed in newspaper, magazine, and broadcast newsrooms across the country.

The news wire services charge a fee for distributing a news release, and the cost of service depends on how long the release is and how wide the distribution is, geographically. The news wires offer an effective though costly method for ensuring that a news release reaches the media on time.

In many cases, the public relations wire services also increase the likelihood that the release will be read. Because editors receive such a large volume of mail each day that often cannot be sorted on a timely basis, most newsrooms assign an individual to monitor the public relations news wires to make sure that important news events are not missed. Releases can be sent to the news wires by messenger or facsimile.

Overnight Mail

Overnight mail services, such as Express Mail, Federal Express, DHL Worldwide, Airborne, and Emery, allow for packages, photos, documents, and other materials to be sent almost anywhere in the world within twenty-four hours.

Overnight mail is a particularly effective method for quickly sending press kits and bulky documents that cannot be transmitted electronically and are too far to send by messenger, but must be delivered within twenty-four hours. One advantage over first-class mail is that people tend to open overnight mail immediately, whereas their first-class mail may sit unopened for hours.

Some overnight services will deliver on Saturday on request, if there will be someone at the receiving address to sign for the package. If you have something that must arrive on Sunday, use the U.S. Postal Service's overnight service.

The drawback is that overnight mail is expensive, costing anywhere from $7 to $30 per package. But it is almost as easy to use as regular mail, and most companies have overnight mail services readily available.

One important thing to remember in using overnight mail is that most services will not deliver to a post office box. A full address and a telephone number are required for guaranteed delivery.

Telephone

In cases of crucial deadlines, releases can be read to a reporter over the telephone. Financial releases in particular—whose timing can influence activity on the stock exchange—are often read over the phone to financial services like the Dow-Jones News Wire or the Reuters Financial Wire.

Most reporters prefer not to have releases read to them over the telephone. Although sometimes this is unavoidable, in most cases, reporters simply do not have the time or patience to listen to a news release.

Electronic Mail

Technology has opened up a new form of document transmission known as electronic mail. Electronic mail is essentially the result of two computers talking with each other through the telephone lines by using modems.

The major drawbacks to electronic mail are the limited number of terminals with modems that are accessible in newsrooms and the inability to transmit photographs.

Summary

The press list is the all-important building block for a public relations campaign. The list must be accurate, up to date, comprehensive, and easy to use. Because public relations professionals are paid to be experts on the media, the press list represents one's knowledge and understanding of the press. An incomplete and sloppy press list, therefore, reflects poorly on the competency of the person who constructed it.

A media list should include the following categories:

- Wire services
- Daily newspapers

- News and general interest publications
- Business publications
- Men's and women's interest magazines
- Primary industry trade publications
- Vertical industry trade publications
- News syndicates and syndicated columnists
- Television and cable
- Radio
- Special interest mailings

Appendix C

Publications

The Production Stage

At the beginning of the editorial process, you decided how many pages your publication would run so that you knew how much copy to write. Most often, the number of pages is decided in multiples of four, because the majority of printing presses work most efficiently on that basis. You can have any number of pages you like, but if you print nine pages, for example, three more will run blank and be discarded, which is wasteful and expensive. So think in terms of designing pages in multiples of four: four pages, eight pages, twelve pages, and so on.

This appendix discusses two approaches to the production of the kinds of publications described in Chapter 8: the traditional methods used for in-house publications and the newer methods of electronic and desktop publishing.

Traditional Production Methods

To go from your manuscript pages to a finished product using traditional means of production, you need to assemble a professional team of an art director, a typesetter, a layout artist, a mechanical artist, a proofreader, a copy editor, and a printer. You can find these team members in several ways. Try reading credits in other publications or asking people you respect in the field if they can refer you to talented and trustworthy professionals.

The art director helps you decide on and gather the art that may accompany the text. Art can mean photographs (referred to as halftones), charts, diagrams, or illustrations. Together, you plan the layout of the publication (referred to as the imposition) and decide what goes where.

The art director also "specs" the copy for typesetting. *Spec* is an abbreviation for "specification," and in this case, speccing a manuscript means marking it for the typesetter with instructions on how it should be set: style of type, margin widths, and so forth.

There are thousands of different "families" of type to choose from, and each typesetting house has different ones available. Typefaces are measured in point sizes.

The art director estimates how many manuscript pages equal one printed page. The ratio depends on the page size and type size. Usually, three double-spaced, typewritten pages equal one typeset, $8\frac{1}{2}$-by-11-inch page using a common typeface and size, such as Times Roman.

After the manuscript is specced and typeset, it is returned to the editor and the art director in the form of galley proofs. The editor proofreads the galleys, as does an outside proofreader, while the art director works on the design of the pages. At this point, copy may have to be cut or adjusted for a perfect fit onto the pages.

There are several reasons that the editor should always hire proofreaders. You can never be trusted to proof your own copy, particularly when you've been "living with it." Professional proofreaders will often find errors or identify problems the editor might not have noticed in the manuscript, and it is in the stages of manuscript and galleys that you want to make any and all corrections.

Galleys should always be marked with standard proofreader's symbols. These symbols are usually listed in dictionaries and stylebooks.

Any galley correction made because of a typesetting mistake is marked in the margin as a PE (printer's error), and there is no charge by the printer for the change. A change made on a correctly typeset galley is marked AA (author's alteration) or EA (editor's alteration), and the editor pays for it. Because AAs and EAs are very costly, the editor tries to make as few as possible, and some publications by contract require a deduction from the author's payment or royalty for AAs. The cost of changes at this stage is another reason that all required approvals should be received before copy is typeset.

Once the galleys have been corrected, the typesetter supplies final "repros" (reproductions) of the typeset copy in a form ready to be pasted down on special boards by a layout artist. Both the art director and the editor guide the layout artist on final layouts.

The printer is often chosen through competitive bidding. That means you find a number of printers who have a reputation for being trustworthy and delivering on time, who are interested in printing your publication, and, above all, whose work you respect. You then submit to all prospective printers a "spec sheet," which, in this case, refers to the specifications of the publication. Price bids are submitted based on the following items on a spec sheet:

Trim size (dimensions of the publication)
Number of pages
Print run (how many printed)
Kind of binding
Number of colors
Frequency printed (how often the publication will be printed)
Supplier of camera-ready mechanicals
Type of paper
Date needed
Place of delivery

Here is a sample spec sheet addressing the above items in printer's language:

Trim size: $8\frac{1}{2}$-by-11 inches
Number of pages: 48
Print run: 50,000
Kind of binding: saddlewire stitch [means binding is stapled; perfect binding means glued]
Number of colors: 4; approximately 60 halftones
Frequency printed: four times a year
Supplier of camera-ready mechanicals: by PR agency
Type of paper: 80-pound, glossy white stock
Date needed: April 1, July 1, November 1, and February 1
Place of delivery: 30,000 mailed from printer to [address]; (remainder delivered to editor)

There may be other steps involved before you go to press. If, for instance, you are printing four-color photos, you will need "color separations," a phrase referring to the process in photography whereby full-color originals are separated into the primary printing colors in negative or positive form.[1]

Proofreading is an ongoing, essential task that does not stop with the correction of galleys. Mechanical boards must also be proofread carefully after the repro copy is pasted down on them. And later, bluelines (test copies made directly from the printing plates, the final stage of production before actual printing) must be proofread. It is very costly and time-consuming to make any changes in bluelines, so at that point, you should, it is hoped, just be checking photo positions and looking for possible broken type.

In many cases, you or the art director will want to be present for press checks to approve when the press is properly adjusted so that the color and alignment of colors (the registration) are at the optimum for each page. Printing and color reproduction are delicate arts, affected by everything from the percentage of moisture in the air and in the paper to the order in which the press applies each color. This careful final press check is eliminated at great risk, unless you have a printer and press operator whose eyes and taste you or your art director respect absolutely.

Electronic and Desktop Publishing

Electronic publishing means using the digital output from computers for as many steps of the publishing process as possible. Electronic publishing can be faster than traditional methods, and it saves time and money. It can also eliminate traditional publishing's potential for creating new typographical errors each time a manuscript must be retyped.

A growing aspect of electronic publishing, desktop publishing means using your personal computer for every stage of the editorial and production processes: writing, editing, design, layout, and printing. Desktop publishing is dependent on having a computer system with capabilities sufficient to your needs and knowing how to use it.

Compatibility and Conversion

The keys to electronic publishing are compatibility and conversion. For example, IBM's and IBM compatibles, which are favored by

[1]International Paper Company, *Pocket Pal: A Graphic Arts Production Handbook,* 220 E 42 St.; NY, NY, 10017, 1979.

many on the editorial side, are just that—compatible with one an-other—and the Macintosh line, which is favored by many graphic designers, was also created for its computers to be compatible with one another. Each year, there are more and more ways to convert material between word processing programs, between Macintosh and IBM systems, and between these systems and high-end prepress systems that create the negatives the printer will use to make the printing plates.

Find an expert to explain exactly what system you or your company should buy or already possess, what capabilities it has with upgrades, and what you must do to make the conversions you need at any step in the editorial and production processes. The cost of the upgrades, conversions, and, if you have to hire a consultant, expert advice will be a factor when you decide which stages to do by traditional means and which to do electronically.

Electronic Publishing and the Editorial Stage

If you use a word processing program for writing and editing, pages do not have to be retyped each time changes are made. If your assigned writer delivers his or her article only on paper, you may edit it on paper. If there are numerous changes, however, you or the writer may have to retype the article before you submit it for approvals, and in any case, it will need to be typeset manually. Each time it is retyped, there is a possibility for new errors, and new rounds of proofreading and retyping will be needed.

In assigning articles, it will, therefore, save you or a secretary the time for retyping if the writer can deliver the assignment on a disk or by modem, in a word processing program that either is compatible with yours or can easily be converted for use with yours.

Electronic Publishing and the Production Stage

Even if you are going to use traditional means for design and layout, you can save time and money by having compatibility or convertibility between your system and the typesetter's. You can then transfer your articles by disk or modem, and the typesetter needs only to input special codes for the different typefaces and sizes, rather than having to retype the entire text.

Doing the design, layout and printing by computer gives you the flexibility to experiment with different typefaces and sizes without the cost and time of going back to the typesetter for new sets of galleys. If you are going to do the design, layout and printing electronically, you have two choices: in-house or out-of-house design.

IN-HOUSE DESIGN. You or someone else can do the design and layout of your publication on your system, but only if your system has a sophisticated enough design program and sufficient memory and other capabilities. Again, you may need to speak with a consultant, and again, you may have to decide if the cost of upgrading is worth the benefits.

If, however, your computer system's design program and printer output are of a quality suitable for your needs, and the number of copies to be printed is not so large that the cost per page becomes prohibitive, you can produce your final publication in-house, right at your desk. This makes you a desktop publisher.

One key to determining the quality of your printer output for the final printed piece is the number of dots per inch (DPI). The printers used with most personal computers have a resolution of 300 DPI, which is adequate for most type but results in poor reproduction of photographs. The output produced by prepress houses is usually 1,200 DPI or higher.

OUT-OF-HOUSE DESIGN. If the design and printing are to be done out-of-house, then you want to have a designer or layout artist who has a compatible system or has conversion capability. By giving the editorial material to the designer by disk or modem, you eliminate the cost and time required for typesetting, and you eliminate both the possibility of new errors and the need for time-consuming and costly new rounds of corrections.

You or your art director must also make sure that the design program and the computer output used by you or the layout artist will be compatible with the system used by the prepress house or printer to make negatives of the layout.

Usually, the prepress house can tell you if and how to link in with their system. Depending on your system and theirs, transfer of data may again be by disk or modem. Only final, proofread, corrected, and approved layouts should be sent to the prepress house.

Any changes from this point on are extremely expensive and time-consuming.

The prepress house may then deliver the complete layout as full-page, reproduction-quality material (repros that look like full-page, glossy galleys), which the printer photographs and makes into negatives. Or, if the prepress house has the capability, it may deliver the output as negatives, one for black and one each for additional custom colors.

The negatives may include the color separations of color photographs, if these have been scanned into the layout; or may be sent to the printer on four separate negatives, for a total of five negatives for each page: process cyan (C), magenta (M), yellow (Y), black (K), and regular black. Included in regular black are the black type and any black and white photographs that may have been scanned into the system electronically.

The printer may then make the negatives into printing plates. If the black-and-white photographs or line drawings have not previously been scanned into the system, the printer may "burn" them directly onto the plate in the designated position, size, and cropping.

Other systems may be able to go directly from the layouts (complete with scanned art) to electronic means of reproduction, including high-end laser and ink-jet printers, depending on the quality of reproduction required, particularly the quality of the photographs, which again depends on the quality of the scanning and the DPI resolution capability of the printer.

Summary

In summary, when producing publications by traditional or electronic means, follow these guidelines:

- Check everything twice—you can never be too careful. Verify information in the manuscript; whenever possible, have professional copyeditors check the manuscript before going into typesetting. Verify photo captions. Assume nothing is correct until you get corroboration from reliable sources.
- Use proven professionals for every phase. Hire art directors and other team members who have experience in the field, can show quality samples of their work, and have good references.

- Get approvals for everything. That applies to copy, art, and layout.
- Keep organized files. Save the originals of copy containing initials of approvals on it; save research files whose sources of information are cited in the copy; and so forth.
- Plan an editorial and production schedule that allows adequate time for each stage to be completed properly.
- Keep in mind that the keys to electronic and desktop publishing are compatibility and convertibility at every stage in the production process. Get expert advice on how you can link your personal computer or office computer to the next stages of the production process and on how to ensure compatibility or convertibility at each step in the production process.

Many public relations jobs center on producing in-house publications. If this process, which requires meticulous attention to detail, appeals to you, you will find it worthwhile to enroll in classes in magazine editing and makeup or in classes in layout and design for electronic or desktop publishing.

Glossary

Actualities Ambient sound; any sound other than that of the primary speaker in a radio or television broadcast.

Annual Report An annual summary of a company's financial condition, prepared for stockholders, and required by the Securities and Exchange Commission for publicly held companies.

Audiovisuals (AV) Graphic presentations that use sight and sound to enhance the understanding of a topic.

Backgrounder Another term for *biography*; gives a client's vital facts and history.

Biography See *backgrounder*.

Businesswire A wire service that runs public relations announcements for a fee (see *PR Newswire*).

Callback A telephone follow-up to a printed invitation or advisory.

Collateral Advertising Product or promotional publications meant to be used with a particular product or service.

Consumer Publication Printed matter intended for the general reader.

Copy Written text.

Corporate Brochure A presentation of a company's distinctive capabilities, often used as a key item in sales, promotions, and media kits.

Daybook Daily schedules of upcoming news events, published by the Associated Press, United Press International, and City News Service.

Delayed Lead A writing style wherein the specific subject of a story doesn't come into clear focus until some time after the first paragraph. The usual intent is to set the background and tone before getting to the main point (compare *inverted pyramid*).

Embargo Any restriction placed on when specific information may be used, often stating the desired date and time of release.

External Newsletter Printed material meant to inform those outside of the company of news and trends happening within it.

Ghostwriting Writing generated without published credit to its author and often credited to another.

In-House Publications Materials generated for perusal within a company—for employees, managers, distributors, and so on. Information in these publications applies directly and exclusively to company matters and would not be of particular interest to outsiders.

Internal Newsletter Printed material meant for those who work within a single company's structure.

Inverted Pyramid A style of writing in which the most comprehensive information is put in the lead, followed by less and less important information; constructed so an editor can cut after any paragraph and have a complete story that meets his or her space limitations.

Lead The introductory sentence or paragraph that summarizes information to follow.

Media Alert Also referred to as a *news advisory* or *tip sheet;* a brief summary of the basic facts surrounding an event, often used when time is too short, or the occasion does not warrant, a printed invitation.

Media Kit An organized package of information that includes background information on general topics or special events.

Media List See *press list.*

Narrowcasting Broadcast journalism that targets audiences with specific interests.

News Advisory See *media alert.*

News Conference An arranged gathering of print and/or broadcast media representatives to announce and explain a significant and newsworthy subject or event.

News Release Also referred to as a *press release;* the most common written form of public relations, used to announce a client's news and information.

Official Statement Also referred to as a *position paper;* a written comment prepared for the purpose of responding consistently to any question from the media regarding a particular controversial issue.

Op-Ed Short for opposite editorial; a newspaper page, usually facing the editorial page, that prints opinions and points of view.

Photo Alert An advisory or invitation that stresses the possibilities for photo coverage.

Pitch Letter A letter to a journalist or editor that introduces a client and story idea or other salient information.

P-O-P Point-of-purchase advertising materials, such as a counter display in a retail store.

Position Paper See *official statement.*

PR Newswire A wire service that runs public relations announcements for a fee (see *Businesswire*).

Press Junket A special tour for news media representatives, in which transportation and accommodations are provided by the company that desires publicity.

Press List Also referred to as a *media list;* a list of targeted press outlets, used for distributing announcements to the press.

Publicity Tour Scheduled publicity appearances in a series of cities or locations, usually developed to publicize books, concerts, or new products or services.

Responsive Writing The act of correcting or capitalizing on a situation by writing to fill in omitted details or otherwise add information that better explains a subject, points out an error, or promotes your client.

Special Event An activity arranged for the purpose of generating publicity.

Stylebook An organization's printed guide to matters of grammar and style.

Target Audience A selected group of people who share similar needs and conditions, such as income, age, sex, or education, and who best represent the most likely potential users of a product or service.

Tease An enticing lead to a story that tells just enough about the story to urge the reader or listener to continue.

Tip Sheet See *media alert.*

Trade Publication A publication that focuses on a specific profession or industry.

Wire Services Companies that supply news to various media on a subscription basis.

Index